*THANKS... AND ENJOY!*

# Lawyer Boy

## A CASE STUDY ON GROWING UP

RICK LAX

*With Illustrations by Steven Katz*

St. Martin's Press ⚮ New York

*www.stmartins.com*

*The drawings in this book are by Steven Katz. The family tree
illustration is by Steven Katz and Linda Lax. The photographs
in the appendixes are by Linda Lax. All are used by permission.*

*Lyrics for the songs "Banana Man," "Welcome to Tally Hall," and
"Two Wuv" by the musical group Tally Hall are reprinted by
permission.*

*Library of Congress Cataloging-in-Publication Data*
Lax, Rick.
    *Lawyer boy : a case study on growing up / Rick Lax.*
        p.   cm.
    ISBN-13: 978-0-312-37335-1
    ISBN-10: 0-312-37335-X
    1. Law students—United States—Anecdotes.   2. Law
students—United States—Humor.   3. Law students—United
States—Fiction.   I. Title.
    KF287.L39 2008
    340.092—dc22                          2008010707

*First Edition: July 2008*

10  9  8  7  6  5  4  3  2  1

*For my parents*

# Contents

## Author's Note

The students and professors described in this book are composites based on my DePaul law school classmates and professors. The character Victoria is also a composite. "Characters" who are not composites include my mother, my father, my childhood buddy Steve, DePaul University College of Law dean Glen Weissenberger, and myself. The character April is not a composite, though her name and identifying characteristics have been changed.

I reconstructed dialogue and altered details of several incidents (e.g., the times and places at which the incidents occurred). The details of certain law school assignments and exam questions have been changed.

In conclusion, please don't sue me.

*Lawyer Boy*

# CHAPTER ONE

## A Sleight Change of Plans

I always wanted to be a magician, but my father, a tax lawyer, never considered magic a "viable career path." My mother, on the other hand, always told me I could do whatever I wanted with my life, but as I grew older, I realized that she and my father were playing Good Cop/Bad Cop and that when she said that I could do whatever I wanted with my life, she meant I could practice whatever kind of law I wanted.

My uncle is a lawyer, and so are my Michigan cousins, my Chicago cousins, and my New York cousins. If I had any siblings, they'd be lawyers, too. My father's father, though, was not a lawyer. He slaughtered cows for a living.[1] Now, I could

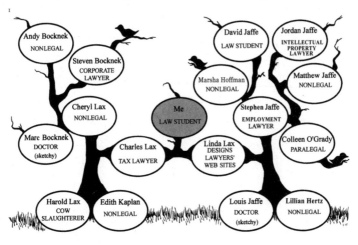

1

easily write half a dozen lawyer jokes comparing slaughter-houses and courtrooms—*they practically write themselves*—but I'm not going to do that because I refuse to disrespect the meatpacking industry—*see?*

All of my friends and ex-girlfriends are lawyers, law students, or soon-to-be law students currently denying their inevitable legal futures. The only exceptions to this rule are (1) my childhood buddy Steve,[2] who works as his dad's law clerk, and (2) my neighbor Stacy, a paralegal. I come from an affluent suburb of Detroit where the only excuse for not practicing law is practicing medicine. But even medicine, many of my dad's partners feel, is a pretty sketchy excuse.

My father and his partners saw my interest in magic the way an evangelical Christian father might view his son's homosexuality. As a *phase*.

"He'll grow out of it," they told my dad.

I imagine one of them took my dad aside and said, "I've never told this to anyone before, but when I was Rick's age, I went through a magic phase, too. My bunkmate showed me my first card trick at summer camp when I was fourteen. . . ."

In middle school, my dad bought me 8.5" × 14" yellow legal pads on which to take notes, the way the evangelical father buys his gay son a baseball glove. But just as the gay son uses the baseball glove as a prop in his school's *Damn Yankees* production, I used the legal pads to sketch blueprints for grand stage illusions. Every time my birthday rolled around,

---

[2] Who did the drawings for this book.

I asked for marked cards and gimmicked coins and linking rings—and received dress shirts, neckties, and dictation recorders. So I sewed secret pockets into the dress shirts, used the neckties for escape demonstrations, and recorded psychic predictions on the dictation recorders (e.g., "Your card was the three of clubs").

I didn't just perform escapes and psychic demonstrations; I performed billiard ball manipulations, rope tricks, and dove illusions.[3] My specialty, though, was performing elaborate, multi-phase card tricks that most professionals wouldn't dare take on, like those of British magician Guy

---

[3] When I was thirteen, I wanted to get two doves to use in my magic act. My parents objected at first but eventually agreed to sign the following contract, which I drew up with a little help from my dad:

BIRD CONTRACT

This agreement made and entered into this 5th day of January, 1996, by and between Richard Lax (hereafter referred to as "Ricky") and Charles and Linda Lax (hereafter collectively referred to as "Mom and Dad").

Whereas, Ricky has expressed a great desire to acquire a pair of doves (hereafter referred to as "Birds"); and

Whereas, Mom and Dad have vehemently objected to such a disgusting acquisition; and

Whereas Mom and Dad believe Ricky is capable of substantially improving his grades; and

Whereas, the parties have agreed that in exchange for better grades as described hereinafter, Ricky will be permitted to acquire the Birds.

Now, therefore, in consideration of the mutual premises and covenants contained herein, it is hereby agreed as follows:

1. Mom and Dad agree that Ricky may, at his own cost and expense, acquire the Birds at any time following receipt of a report
*(continued on next page)*

Hollingworth. Hollingworth created one of my favorite card tricks, *Reformation,* in which a signed playing card is torn into four and then restored, piece by piece. It sounds simple, but it isn't; the trick's explanation goes on for thirty-six pages and contains instructions like this:

> The front edge of the left hand's card should be in contact with the front of the right's, so that when the cards are directly aligned with each other, that front edge can slide in between the right fingers and the other cards, so

---

card upon which he obtains a grade of "A+," "A," or "A−" in the following subjects: Math, Science, English, and Social Studies (hereafter referred to as "Academic Subjects").

2. Mom and Dad further agree that Ricky may, at his own cost and expense, acquire the Birds following receipt of his report card in June of 1996, in the event that Ricky meets with a tutor, principally for Math, but possibly for other Academic Subjects, as the parties may mutually agree, at least once a week from the date of the signing of this contract until the receipt of Ricky's June of 1996 report card, subject to the availability of both Ricky and the Tutor. For the purposes of this contract, Ricky and the Tutor will be deemed unavailable: (i) in the event that either is out of town, (ii) in the event that either is ill, or (iii) in the event that a matter of greater importance, *as designated such by Mom and Dad,* comes up.

Richard Lax

Charles M. Lax

Linda S. Lax

that the right hand holds it in place; meanwhile the left thumb is still holding the other side of the folded V-shaped card, and immediately moves upwards, unfolding the card; at the same time the left fingers move to the side, so that the card is seen as it is being opened.[4]

As a teenager, I fantasized about creating illusions so elaborate they'd make Guy Hollingworth's *Reformation* look like Dan Harlan's *Card-Toon* (!),[5] so you can imagine how betrayed I felt when, at the age of twenty-four, Hollingworth left the field of magic to study law.

Hollingworth's career change got me thinking: maybe practicing law isn't all that different from performing magic. The most powerful weapon in both lawyers' and magicians' arsenals is misdirection; just as Slydini misdirected an audience's attention away from the billiard ball's true location (Slydini's right hand) by looking at his left hand, Johnnie Cochran misdirected jurors' attention away from the DNA evidence by focusing on the pair of ill-fitting Isotoners.

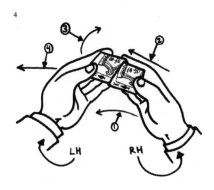

4

[5] If you were a magician, you'd be laughing really hard right now.

The main difference between magicians and lawyers is that lawyers have no use for sleight of hand. This difference is as personally disappointing as it is obvious—for every hour my dad spent pacing around the kitchen, saying things like "bargained-for consideration" and "promissory estoppel" into his dictation recorder, I'd spent three in front of the bathroom mirror practicing rope sleights.

"Judges," my father once told me, "aren't impressed by lawyers who can tie four varieties of slipknots; the only knots judges like are the ones that go around lawyers' necks."

My father wasn't referring to a noose—my father doesn't make lawyer jokes—he was referring to neckties, and the reason he was referring to neckties was that I couldn't tie one. I'd always figured that if I never learned how to tie a necktie, nobody could rationally expect me to hold down a desk job. Unfortunately, I overestimated society's rationality, because *everybody* expected me to hold down a desk job. Specifically, society expected me to become a lawyer—this much was made clear to me while I was sitting shivah for my grandfather.

"Have you thought about law school? I bet that'd make your dad real happy."

*You think?*

"I'd love to take you out for lunch so we could talk about law school—your dad told me you're thinking of going."

*He did? I am?*

"I heard your big news!"

*I didn't.*

"Law school!"

*Law school?*

"What a smart decision."

*Uh . . . thanks. . . .*

"Your grandfather would be so proud. I didn't want to tell you this until you made a final decision, but your grandfather always wanted you to become a lawyer like your father."

*No pressure or anything.*

Before my grandfather's funeral, my father sat me down at the kitchen table and said, "It's time for you to learn how to tie a tie." My father had offered to teach me how to tie a tie before every wedding, bar mitzvah, and funeral, and I'd always declined—that was the ritual. Only this time, my father wasn't joking around. "It's time for you to learn. Really." Maybe my grandfather's death had gotten my father thinking about how he wouldn't always be around to teach me how to do it. But when I declined again, my father did the same thing he had done my entire life: he tied my tie on himself, slipped it off his neck, and placed it around mine.

In terms of employability, political science degrees make English degrees look like business degrees. Politics isn't a science, and therefore there's no such thing as a political scientist, and therefore poli-sci students generally need to find other fields to actually enter upon graduation. At the University of Michigan, my poli-sci classmates swore they'd never go into teaching political science, but fraternity pledges say the same thing about abolishing hazing once they become upperclassmen. And yet, year after year, the ridiculous, pointless rituals continue, as does fraternity hazing.

After graduation I moved back in with my parents, where the closest thing I had to a job was watching *The Price Is Right,* in that I had to make it to the living room couch at the same time every day. A master of the art of reverse psychology, my mother enthused about having me back: "I feel so fortunate to spend all this time with you."

I found her lies insultingly transparent.

Unemployment isn't as easy as you'd think. As an unemployee, you often struggle with the desire to *do something,* and fighting that desire off requires fortitude and focus. On the plus side, you have plenty of time to surf the Internet, watch decades-old *Magic of David Copperfield* VHS tapes, go to Dunkin' Donuts with your high school buddies, and date the same girls you dated in high school, the main difference being that these girls are now less likely to go to second base with you because they fail to appreciate the fortitude and focus required to not do anything. Dating new girls isn't really an option, either (e.g., "Want to come back to my place . . . and meet my parents?").

I didn't just live with my parents. I watched their televisions, drove their cars, and wore their clothes when mine were dirty and I was too lazy to wash them and too lazy to ask my mom to wash them for me.

I didn't appreciate how dependent I'd become until the night my father flew to Washington for a business meeting and I needed him to tie my tie. At that time, I was playing cowbell for my friend Rob's rock band Tally Hall in their song "Banana Man."[6] Tally Hall always wore neckties when performing, and as their cowbellist, I was expected to wear one, too. Only I couldn't because I didn't know how to tie one and wouldn't admit that to the guys in the band. So I took to the stage with my dress shirt unbuttoned and untucked. Two-thirds of the way through the song, I missed one of my cues. I was preoccupied by the following thought: *I'm twenty-two years old, not retarded, and I still need my daddy to dress me.*

I realized that my full-time immaturity shtick would one day inevitably turn from cute and charming to sad and creepy. I realized that I couldn't live with my parents forever, that I needed a place of my own, and that magic wouldn't pay the bills—the ones I'd presumably have if I had a place of my own. I realized that I had to go to law school . . . because it's not like I was going to get a job or anything.

The Law School Admission Test is a five-hour multiple-choice exam administered to provide a "standard measure of acquired reading and verbal reasoning skills that law schools can use as one of several factors in assessing applicants," and to crush the aspirations of twentysomethings who grew up

[6] *Do you see Banana Man*
*Hopping over on de white-hot sand?*
*Here he come with some for me,*
*Freshly taken from banana tree.*

*Banana Man me want a ton.*
*Give me double and a bonus one.*
*Give me more for all me friends.*
*Dis banana flow will never end.*

watching *Law & Order* thinking, *That looks cool. I can do that.* These twentysomethings are largely wrong—they can't do that. To make that point perfectly clear, the Law School Admission Committee designed the LSAT so that the average test taker (one who scores at the fiftieth percentile) can't even complete the exam in the given time. Of course, half of all LSAT takers receive below average scores,[7] and for that half the chances of admission are not good. But not to worry, *Law & Order* fans, according to one undergraduate school's Web site:

> There are at least two accredited law schools in the nation that will take almost anyone, offering them the chance at law school, but nothing more. These schools tend to flunk out 75% of their students after the first year, taking their tuition and sending them off. But if you can hack it, you can stay.

[7] LSAT SCORE TO PERCENTILE CONVERSION CHART

| SCORE | PERCENTILE | SCORE | PERCENTILE |
|-------|-----------|-------|-----------|
| 180 | 99.9 | 145 | 28.4 |
| 175 | 99.7 | 140 | 14.6 |
| 170 | 98.2 | 135 | 6.3 |
| 165 | 93.5 | 130 | 2.3 |
| 160 | 83 | 125 | 0.8 |
| 155 | 67 | 120 | 0 |
| 150 | 47.2 | | |

Students with low LSAT scores can also enroll in nonaccredited law schools, but I don't know why they'd want to; most states—California being the most notable exception—won't even allow graduates of nonaccredited law schools to take the bar exam. According to The Princeton Review, law schools not accredited by the American Bar Association have other problems:

> Some critics argue that schools not accredited by the ABA are oriented less towards instilling students with a thorough knowledge of the law, and more towards teaching them how to pass the bar exam, supplying part-time professors and Spartan facilities. Two years ago, approximately eighty percent of students who attended ABA-approved schools in California passed the bar exam, versus approximately thirty percent for students who attended [California Bar Association]–approved schools, and about fifteen percent for those who went the non-accredited route.

The Princeton Review also says: "Many people feel that they have to score at least a 160 to get into a 'good' law school. That's pure myth." When translated from motivational test–prep puffery to prospective law studentese, that means: "If you don't score at least a 160, you are a failure—not just as a prospective law student, but as a human being. Nobody could ever love an idiot like you." Unlike the SAT, if you get a bad LSAT score, you can't take the test a second time without consequence. Law schools are given access to your complete record, not just your highest score.

My father doesn't remember his LSAT score—allegedly—but it was high enough to earn him a seat at the University of Michigan Law School. The University of Michigan doesn't just have the best law school in Michigan; it has one of the best in the country. The law school shows up on the *U.S. News & World Report* top-ten ranking every year.[8] The median starting salary of 2007 graduates was $125,000.

If I did well on the LSAT, I'd earn a seat at the University of Michigan Law School, my ticket to the six-figure job, gas-guzzling SUV, and ungrateful trophy wife of my dreams. If I did poorly, I'd have to blow my (parents') hard-earned money at a California diploma mill for the tiny chance that I might pass the bar and find a job defending indigent baby rapists.

Getting into the University of Michigan's undergraduate program was tough—I'd needed to transfer in. Getting into their law school, I recognized, would be almost impossible. The Supreme Court made that much clear in the 2003 case *Grutter v. Bollinger*. The case's *opinion*[9] begins: "The [University of Michigan] Law School ranks among the Nation's top law schools. It receives more than 3,500 applications each year for a class of around 350 students." In *Grutter,* the Supreme Court held that state universities have a compelling interest in obtaining the educational benefits that flow from a

[8] The ranking is based on opinion surveys, incoming student profiles, acceptance rates, placement success, bar passage rates, expenditures, library volumes, and student/faculty ratios.

[9] *Opinion:* the document in which a judge explains why she ruled the way she did.

diverse student body, and that this interest justifies the use of race as a factor in admissions. But even without affirmative action, plaintiff Barbara Grutter, who had a 3.8 GPA and 161 LSAT score, probably couldn't get into the University of Michigan Law School today. In recent years, the average incoming University of Michigan Law School student has had a 3.7 GPA and 168 LSAT score.

Coming out of college, I didn't have a 3.7 GPA. The As I earned in Choir I, Choir II, Acting I, Acting II, Experimental Composition, and Creative Writing barely pulled my GPA above a 3.4. I would need a sky-high LSAT score to guarantee myself a seat at my father's law school.

According to the American Bar Association, when my father began his legal education in 1968, there were just 3,554 women enrolled in ABA-accredited schools; in 2005, there were 66,613. In 1971, just 5,568 minority students attended ABA-accredited law schools; in 2005, 29,768 did.[10] There's a good chance my father couldn't get into the University of Michigan Law School today with his old scores. But that's the kind of sound-minded evaluation that can only be done in retrospect; before I took the LSAT, all I knew was that I had to score at least a 170 so I could get into my father's law school, or else, like scientist George Darwin, I'd be forever doomed to work in my father's professional shadow.

The biggest obstacle standing in the way of my getting a spectacular LSAT score was my mediocre test-taking ability, as evidenced by my mediocre GPA. The best thing I had

[10] The ABA statistics for minority enrollment begin in 1971.

going for me was all the free time I had to attend LSAT prep classes like Kaplan, which boasted a "unique combination of the highest quality study materials, realistic testing experiences, and dynamic teachers and tutors"; The Princeton Review, which promised to help me "master LSAT content, build skills with practice tests, and learn proven test-taking strategies"; and PowerScore, which claimed to provide me with "the maximum exposure to the concepts that appear on the LSAT, access to the best possible instructors and classroom material, and the best support system to augment [my] studies." I could easily fit all three into my schedule and still have time to not get a job.

In *Barrel Fever,* David Sedaris wrote: "The truly crazy are labeled so on the grounds that they see nothing wrong with their behavior."[11] Similarly, truly bad test takers don't grasp how bad they are at taking tests until they get their grades back. If they knew how poorly they were going to do, they would study harder. That's the best way I can explain my decision not to take any LSAT review courses.

I might justify my decision by saying (1) I did well on the SAT, (2) the LSAT is just one letter away, (3) my ex–workout buddy, who got into a prestigious California law school—a prestigious *ABA-accredited* California law school—told me that the LSAT and SAT are "pretty much the same test," and (4) I believed him.

---

[11] "They forge ahead, lighting fires in public buildings and defecating in frying pans without the slightest notion that they are out of step with the rest of society. That, to me, is crazy. Calling yourself crazy is not crazy, only obnoxious."

Unfortunately, in making my decision I failed to consider that (1) my parents forced me to take a Princeton Review course before the SAT, (2) the course greatly improved my SAT score, and (3) the reason I stopped working out with my ex–workout buddy was that I couldn't tolerate his habitual lying.

A few weeks after the LSAT review course sign-up dates had passed, my daily Internet surfing session brought me to lsac.org, which offered the complete October 1996 LSAT. I downloaded and printed the test, found my mom's old egg timer in the drawer under the stove, set it for thirty-five minutes, began the first section, and quickly cursed my ex–workout buddy for the liar he was.

Here are two sample SAT—not LSAT—questions taken from the College Board's *Official SAT Study Guide*. The College Board gives test takers roughly sixty seconds to answer each question, so start your timers and **BEGIN NOW**:

Question 1:
He displayed a nearly pathological _____, insisting on knowing every detail of his friends' lives.
(A) orderliness
(B) credulity
(C) curiosity
(D) shyness
(E) morbidity

Question 2:
Efforts are finally being made to _____ the traffic congestion that plagues the downtown area.

(A) engage

(B) alleviate

(C) transport

(D) regenerate

(E) trivialize

**STOP**. Put down your pencil. The answer to the first question is C, and the answer to the second question is B, and if you're smart enough to read this book, you knew that already.

Now, try your hand at two questions taken from the October 1996 LSAT. Test takers get about ninety seconds to answer each question, so, once again, start your timers and **BEGIN NOW:**

Question 1:

No one in the French department to which Professor Alban belongs is allowed to teach more than one introductory level class in any one term. Moreover, the only language classes being taught next term are advanced ones. So it is untrue that both of the French classes Professor Alban will be teaching next term will be introductory level classes.

**The pattern of reasoning displayed in the argument above is most closely paralleled by that in which one of the following arguments?**

(A) The Morrison Building will be fully occupied by May and since if a building is occupied by May the new tax rates apply to it, the Morrison Building will be taxed according to the new rates.

(B) The revised tax code does not apply at all to buildings built before 1900, and only the first section of the revised code applies to buildings built between 1900 and 1920, so the revised code does not apply to the Norton Building, since it was built in 1873.

(C) All property on Overton Road will be reassessed for tax purposes by the end of the year and the Elnor Company headquarters is on Overton Road, so Elnor's property taxes will be higher next year.

(D) New buildings that include public space are exempt from city taxes for two years and all new buildings in the city's Alton district are exempt for five years, so the building with the large public space that was recently completed in Alton will not be subject to city taxes next year.

(E) Since according to recent statute, a building that is exempt from property taxes is charged for city water at a special rate, and hospitals are exempt from property taxes, Founder's Hospital will be charged for city water at the special rate.

Question 2:

At an evening concert, a total of six songs—O, P, T, X, Y, and Z—will be performed by three vocalists— George, Helen, and Leslie. The songs will be sung consecutively as solos, and each will be performed exactly once. The following constraints govern the composition of the concert program:

- Y must be performed earlier than T and earlier than O.
- P must be performed earlier than Z and later than O.
- George can perform only X, Y, and Z.
- Helen can perform only T, P, and X.
- Leslie can perform only O, P, and X.
- The vocalist who performs first must be different from the vocalist who performs last.
- If Y is performed first, the songs performed second, third, and fourth, respectively, could be—

(A) T, X, and O
(B) T, Z, and O
(C) X, O, and P
(D) X, P, and Z
(E) X, T, and O


**STOP**. Put your pencils down.


The only thing those LSAT questions have in common with the SAT questions earlier is the number of answer choices. The best thing I can say about my overall performance on the October 1996 LSAT is that I didn't cry. And while I didn't score a 170, my score did have a 1 and a 7 in it.

147.
*California, here I come.*


Though it was too late to take the Kaplan or Princeton Review prep courses, it wasn't too late to go through their respective study guides. The local Barnes & Noble had an entire shelf of LSAT prep books (e.g., the *Arco 30 Days to the LSAT: Teacher-Tested Strategies and Techniques for Scoring High,* the *PowerScore LSAT Logic Games Bible, 10 Actual, Official LSAT PrepTests, 10 More Actual, Official LSAT PrepTests*), and I bought four of them. I schlepped the books to the store's café, plopped the pile on the table, and began at the beginning.

The maddeningly upbeat *Barron's* LSAT book kicked things off with a keyed-up "Good Luck!!!" I'd need every one of those three motivational exclamation points to get me through the study guide's seven hundred pages of tips, tricks, and sample exams. *Barron's LSAT* classified LSAT problems into categories like "Inferences and Implications" and "Parallel Reasoning or Similarity of Logic." The Princeton Review's *Cracking the LSAT* problem categories sounded much less scientific (i.e., "Weaken" and "Flaw"), as did the following instruction:

Suppose you wished to support the following conclusion of an argument:

Driving stupidly is permitted.

Given two forms of answer choices—blah blah blah is permitted *if* versus blah blah blah is permitted *only if*—it's clear that only the first will do.

If *Barron's* informal punctuation and *Princeton Review*'s casual tone lulled me into a false sense of confidence, it didn't last long—Kaplan saw to that. Kaplan's *LSAT 180* began: "We should warn you up front: This book is not for the faint of heart." Kaplan wasn't messing around. Going through Kaplan's *LSAT 180* was like altitude training; the problems were way harder than any that would be on a real LSAT exam. Here's an example:

Question 1:
There are those, Mr. Hobbes foremost among them, who maintain that before any positive laws were instituted, there could be no distinction between the good and the evil, the just and the unjust. In the state of nature, each had the "right" to lop off the head of any other. This frightening situation prompted those in a state of nature to form a social body and enact positive laws that forbid murder. It was only with the formation of these laws that good and evil were born; and it was only as a result of these laws that murder could be termed evil. This description is inaccurate. If murder was deemed so unfit and unreasonable an act that men entered into contracts to preserve themselves, then murder must have been understood as unfit and unreasonable before such contracts were formed. This being the case, these thinkers' supposition that there is neither "good" nor "evil" antecedent to the institution of law is self-defeating: If the distinction between good and evil is once admitted to exist, then it has always.

**The author intends to discredit the view of Mr. Hobbes and similar thinkers by attempting to:**

(A) present historical evidence in support of his view
(B) show that their argument contains circular reasoning
(C) show that their account of the origin of morality presupposes a contradiction

(D) point out the unacceptable consequences of their view on mortality

(E) impugn the motives of these thinkers themselves, rather than dealing with their argument.[12]

All but the last of those answer choices sounded good to me. I felt comfortable making arguments for each of them. But maybe that wasn't such a bad thing; as a lawyer, I'd have to make arguments on behalf of whoever walked through my door. So wasn't it then a testament to my professional capabilities that I felt equally comfortable defending the correct and incorrect answer choices?

I returned to Barnes & Noble day after day to study, and after two weeks, two things happened: (1) some answer choices began to look more correct than others, and (2) I started to feel as though I had a real job.[13] When my coworkers (e.g., the Chaldean guy studying for the GRE, the Holocaust survivor who read newspapers and looked like my deceased grandfather [if my deceased grandfather were six inches shorter—and still alive], the girl who always acted as if I were hitting on her, even though I wasn't because I would never hit on anyone reading books from the New Age

[12] According to *LSAT 180,* the author of this passage does not present historical evidence, employ circular logic, make moral arguments, or unleash ad hominem attacks. "The author believes, thinkers such as Hobbes assume *first,* that the state of nature *is* free of moral judgment, and *second,* that this state is *not* free of moral judgment." Therefore, choice C is correct.

[13] Though no more real than my *Price Is Right* watching gig in terms of dollars and cents.

section) asked me how I was doing, I'd reply, "Another Monday," or, "Weekend's coming up," which, having spent the summer of my junior year photocopying case files at my father's office, I'd learned, is what having a real job is all about.

Some days I memorized LSAT tips and tricks; others I took timed practice exam sections, which was tough because my coworkers didn't think twice about waltzing into my office (i.e., walking by my table) and striking up a conversation whenever they saw fit.

"Working hard?" they'd ask.

"I'm trying."

"You're studying for that law school test, right?"

"I was."

"Well, I'll let you get back to that."

"Thanks."

"I'll just be on my way."

"See you around."

"Say, when is the test?"

To properly practice for the LSAT—according to every LSAT prep book ever published, anyway—I would need to get through each timed practice section uninterrupted.

Five days before the test, I took an entire practice exam at my father's office. It was the ideal location: it had soundproof conference rooms and an amply stocked kitchen. My father works at a midsized Detroit law firm called Maddin, Hauser. Michael Maddin and Mark Hauser both still practice. Michael Maddin's son Marty works at Maddin, Hauser, and so does Mark Hauser's son Michael.

Starting to see a pattern with this stuff yet?

When I told my dad that I had scored a 169, you could have knocked him over with a feather.

Three days before the LSAT, I took one last practice exam—this one at home. Halfway through the second section, Rob from Tally Hall called me up and asked if I could help the band out for an hour.[14]

"I've got to take a practice LSAT," I replied. "It's going to take all afternoon."

"We really need your help for this publicity shot. We need you to put this medieval suit of armor on and walk out of a Porta-Potty."

Because I had already dressed up as a gorilla and as a chicken for the band, I couldn't claim to be above playing dress-up,[15] so I just said, "Can't do it today. Sorry, buddy."

"Guess we'll find somebody else," Rob said, a little too quickly, as if he were trying to lure me in with that damned reverse psychology.

"Guess so," I replied.[16]

---

[14] When a musician says he needs your help for "an hour," he means that he needs your help for four hours. ($AH = RH \times 3 + 1$. [$AH =$ Actual Hours, $RH =$ Requested Hours]). Incidentally, the formula for undergraduate film major time requests is $AH = RH \times 4.5 + 2 +$ "Do you think you could come by for like forty-five minutes tomorrow so we could finish this thing up?"

[15] The Model Rules of Professional Conduct forbid lawyers from making misstatements of material fact.

[16] Rob knew what I was going through; he had taken the MCAT a few months earlier. His score earned him a full-ride scholarship to the University of Michigan, which he turned down, so he could stay with the band. Did I mention his father is a doctor?

And so began a new direction in my life—one that prioritized scholarship over bathroom humor.

Two days and counting. I needed a study break, so my parents and I went to see the touring production of *Copenhagen,* Michael Frayn's play about a meeting between physicists Niels Bohr and Werner Heisenberg. Each of the play's three acts recounts the same meeting. The play's only stage directions, I presume, are "speak" and "speak while walking in a circle." There are only three actors and no scene changes.

We saw the play at Detroit's historic Fisher Theatre, where a few dozen audience members, my family included, were selected to sit on two rows of wooden rafters framing the stage for the duration of the performance. I think the theater as a whole was intended to represent an atom, the actors being electrons circling the nucleus (hence the circle walking).[17]

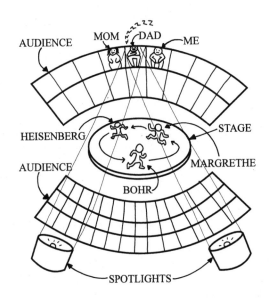

[17]

AUDIENCE   MOM   DAD   ME

HEISENBERG   STAGE

AUDIENCE   MARGRETHE

BOHR

SPOTLIGHTS

Even with the Fisher Theatre's massive spotlights shining right in my father's eyes and even with 2,008 Fisher Theatre patrons staring right at him, my father slept throughout most of the play's second act and all of its third, excluding the nuclear explosion at the end.

After graduating from college, I typically fell asleep around four, only two hours before my father's alarm went off. But as the preceding anecdote should illustrate, my father's sleep schedule was no healthier than mine.[18] My dad would come home every night with a heaping pile of files to read, mark up, and leave on the kitchen table for my mother and me to spill red wine on. When he'd finished working, he could fall asleep on any couch, chair, or stool he found himself on.

After *Copenhagen*, we drove home and my father drank a big glass of ice water to wake himself up and then worked until one on a small business owner's pension plan. My dad fell asleep around two and woke up for work the following morning before six. The point is, though he didn't sleep much—in his bed, at least—I could trust him to wake me up on the day of the test.[19]

When only two contenders remain in a poker tournament, the organizers dump the contended cash on the table to remind both players what's at stake. In the same way, the LSAC administers the LSAT at the University of Michigan Law School.

[18] If your attorney tells you she has a healthy, regular sleep schedule, you need to report her to the Attorney Registration & Disciplinary Commission immediately; if nothing troubling is keeping her awake at night, she's not doing her job with due diligence.

[19] I couldn't rely on my alarm clock because I'm a snooze junkie.

The test would begin at 8:30 A.M., which meant that I would need to show up at the school at 8:00 A.M., which meant that I would need to be in Ann Arbor at 7:30 A.M. to guarantee myself a parking spot, which meant that I would need to leave West Bloomfield by 6:45 A.M., which meant that my father would need to wake me up at 5:45 A.M., which, as I've said, was not quite two hours past my bedtime.

The night before the LSAT, I climbed into bed around eleven. At midnight, I climbed out, drank two glasses of red wine, and then got back in. At one, I considered pulling an all-nighter. Getting two or three hours of sleep, I reasoned, might be worse than getting none. By 1:15 A.M., I had decided that an all-nighter was definitely the way to go. By 1:30 A.M., once I had committed myself to not falling asleep, I fell asleep.

My dad woke me up at 5:45 A.M. ("Time to get up"), and then again at 6:00 A.M. ("Okay, I gave you fifteen minutes"), and then again at 6:10 A.M. ("Do you even want to do this, or should I just let you sleep through it?"). Damn reverse psychology. Works every time. I was up. By 8:15 A.M., I had made it to the University of Michigan Law School campus, a few acres of gorgeous Gothic architecture, which I was way too tired to appreciate. I stood in line with a few hundred of my peers to get a seat assignment. I was nervous but also too tired to manifest my nervousness. I couldn't find the energy to pace or even tap my foot.

I recognized many of the test takers, and not just from the University of Michigan poli-sci department, although everybody in the poli-sci department was there. Many of my high school classmates, classmates who had never struck me as the legal type, had apparently been harboring *Law & Order* dreams of their own. Like Becky, who acted like a Valley Girl impersonating a Valley Girl (even though our high school was located over two thousand miles from the San Fernando Valley), and Rod, who was best known for scoring a hat trick of 5s on his AP Chemistry, AP Physics, and AP Calculus BC exams (a feat far more impressive than scoring a 170 on the LSAT) and for pulling his pants down behind the backs of substitute teachers.

Before the exam, representatives of *The Princeton Review* brought goodie bags to their LSAT prep course graduates. The bags contained inspirational messages, several pieces of candy, and some No. 2 pencils. Finally, I made it to the front of the line, where a proctor showed me to my assigned seat, which was next to that of a girl wearing sorority sweatpants and a Chris Perry football jersey.

"You ready?" I asked.

She nodded and then looked away. She was in no mood to talk; she was in the zone. So I continued the conversation, hoping to throw her off her game, thus bringing down her score, thus increasing the relative worth of mine.

"Did you take a review course?" I asked, even though I already knew she did because I had seen her putting a *Princeton Review* goodie bag in her backpack.

She squeezed her pencil in frustration. My strategy was working. She said that, yes, she did take a review course, and that all of her sorority sisters had taken courses as well, except for Chesca, her sorority's president, who was only taking the LSAT to give her mother, a state judge, numeric proof of how unlikely it was that Chesca would follow in her footsteps. It's that kind of "who cares?" attitude that quiets the nerves and practically guarantees success. Chesca probably scored a 180.

Halfway through the proctor's introductory comments, I felt the need to relieve myself. The proctor told us to pick up our pencils and begin the first section, so I did, hoping the proctor would give us a break between the first two sections.

She didn't.

The second section was particularly tough, but when you have to urinate as badly as I did, anything except for urinating is tough. When the second section ended, the administrator told us to put our pencils down.

"You may now take a two-minute break," she announced. "You are not permitted to discuss any aspects of the test with each other." I ran out of the room, down the hallway, down the stairs, past the lockers, into the bathroom, and back, in record time, but everyone had already begun the third section by the time I returned.

"Time's up," the proctor announced at the end of the third section. "Put your pencils down. There will be a fifteen-minute break. You are encouraged to use the bathroom during this time."

Like the practice LSAT, I got through the real thing without crying. Everybody did. We were fidgety at the start, but eventually the coughing and throat clearing and pencil tapping stopped and everybody got down to business.

The LSAC Web site told me I'd get my score back in approximately three weeks. My mom suggested I find a project to keep my mind off my LSAT score, which, she pointed out, I could no longer affect. So I got to work obtaining letters of recommendation. The University of Michigan allows students to submit up to four letters of recommendation. Every law school prep book I read said that when it comes to letters of recommendation, "allows" means "requires."

My first letter came from Ralph Williams, my undergraduate Bible in the English Language professor. The people on the University of Michigan Law School admissions committee definitely knew who he was; he had won the *Michigan Daily*'s Best Professor award nine of the last ten years. This professor had (once) adored me, but I was nervous about asking him to write me a letter of recommendation because our last interaction hadn't ended well: I'd interviewed him on behalf of *The Michigan Daily* and my editor ran the article under the headline "Professor Exposes It All," which made it sound like the guy took his pants off during our interview.

Professor Williams canceled our initial meeting due to a literary emergency: he had to fly to England to help Salman Rushdie work out some last-minute kinks on an upcoming stage adaptation of *Midnight's Children*. So we met the following week. After reading several of my undergraduate papers and interrogating me as to why I wanted to go into law,

Williams agreed to write my first letter of recommendation. He even got Rushdie to edit it.

Not really, but that would have been cool.

For my second letter, I approached my high school drama teacher. A high school drama teacher isn't the most obvious choice for a law school recommendation, but she thought I was an artistic genius, and for recommendations, enthusiasm counts. I found her onstage leading a dozen kids through an improvisational exercise that involved crying, hugging, and apologizing. She noticed me standing in the back of the theater and introduced me as "one of the finest actors to have ever mounted the Andover stage."[20] Naturally, she agreed to write my second letter of recommendation.

Once I had my recommendation momentum going, I had no problem securing my third and fourth letters from my Comparative Politics and Creative Writing professors.

Then I received an e-mail from the LSAC. *The* e-mail.

I got a 163 out of 180—89.9th percentile.

I wouldn't have to buy that one-way California ticket after all. My chances of University of Michigan Law School admission, though, were not good. I'd needed a 170 to guarantee myself a seat, and I'd fallen seven points short. So after I sent in the U-of-M application, I applied elsewhere,

[20] I went to Andover High School in Bloomfield Hills, Michigan. It's a public school—not to be confused with Phillips Andover, the private preparatory school in Andover, Massachusetts, once attended by George W. Bush.

which wasn't easy for me; the only school I had ever imagined myself attending was my father's. First I applied to the William S. Boyd School of Law at the University of Nevada, Las Vegas, then the DePaul University College of Law in Chicago, schools that, given my numbers, I would probably get into. I also applied to the University of Chicago Law School, the New York University School of Law, and Columbia Law School—three schools to which I'd only be admitted in the event of a clerical error. But for a couple hundred (of my parents') dollars in application fees that was a chance I was willing (i.e., allowed, per my parents' approval) to take. Still, U-of-M was my number-one choice.

The next week, in a misguided attempt to distract me from the admission results, my father began to tell me law school horror stories. I learned about the Socratic Method of teaching, in which a professor calls upon a random student and asks her to state the facts of a case. The student does so, and then the professor asks a series of increasingly complex questions until (1) the student correctly identifies the main issues of the case and the judge's opinion on those issues, (2) the student tears a page from her book and waves it as a white flag, or (3) the class brownnoser calls out the correct answer, relieving the first student of her impending doom and confirming his position as class brownnoser.

My father went into the garage and pulled out a dusty, gray, thirty-five-year-old law school folder. He showed me one of his marked-up legal writing papers:

"You have negligence and malpractice hopelessly confused."

"Your sentences are often unintelligible and consistently show poor grammar."

"This brief exhibits a shallowness of preparation and a lack of familiarity with the basic approach to legal writing sufficient to make me think you didn't try very hard."

He said it was one of his good papers.

My dad also suggested that I read *One L,* Scott Turow's 1977 book about his first year at Harvard Law School. Fifty pages in, I understood why my father had waited until after I'd submitted my applications: I've read three Stephen King novels, one book on exorcism, and one on delusional paranoid schizophrenia, and *One L* was easily scarier than all of them put together.

Turow, who'd felt overwhelmed and intellectually inadequate throughout his first year, had an LSAT score in the 99th percentile. If law school scared a genius like him, I could only imagine what it would do to an 89th percentilian like me.


Envelope size takes all the drama out of application results. If you get a big, chunky envelope from the school of your choice, congratulations, you're in. If you get a measly #10, you're not. In the movies, schools use #10 envelopes for rejections and acceptances so the characters don't know whether they've been accepted until they ask their best friend (who's secretly in love with them and doesn't want them to leave their hometown for the big city but still feigns enthusiasm) to open the envelope because they're just too nervous.[21]

I received rejections from the University of Chicago, NYU, and Columbia that went something like this:

Dear Rick Lax,

Thank you for applying to The _____ Law School. Of the thousands who apply each year, we can only select a few hundred, and let's just say, you're not one of them. However, your college transcript, LSAT score, and personal essay gave the Admissions Committee the laugh we needed to lighten the painstaking process of sorting through the real applicants. For that, we thank you.

But you should have seen our faces when we saw your junior year grades. We were like, "Whoa! Whaaa ha ha! Tee hee hee hee! Hee hee hee heeeeee!" Good times.

To return the favor, we considered sending you a plain white postcard with "NO" stamped on it in red capital letters, but decided it would be funnier to send you the rejection letter you're reading now in one of our acceptance envelopes. That way, when you saw it, you'd

---

[21] *The OC* corrected this in Season 3, Episode 20, "The Day After Tomorrow," during which the kids received appropriately sized college acceptance and rejection letters.

think you got in, only to then feel the sudden, crushing disappointment that is the reality of your own feeble-mindedness.

> We hate you,
> The _____ Law School

As expected, the University of Las Vegas accepted me, and even threw in a $9,000 annual scholarship. DePaul University College of Law in Chicago trumped that with an $18,000-a-year offer, accompanied by a 100 percent cotton XL school T-shirt.

*So this is what Kobe Bryant missed out on when he skipped college.*

The University of Michigan Law School letter showed up last, and it showed up in a #10 envelope. That envelope contained the best news a #10 envelope could: I had made the waiting list. But so had Barbara Grutter (of *Grutter v. Bollinger*). Grutter sued the school, which didn't work, so I tried using a connection—a University of Michigan Law School donor who just happened to be my father's friend's sister's friend. I called the woman up and invited her to breakfast. I charmed and flattered her over pancakes before asking her to put in a good word for me with the admissions committee.

"I'd be delighted to," she said. "I think the school would benefit from having more students with your passion and optimism."

Her use of the word "optimism" scared me. *Am I optimistic to think our breakfast might actually get me off the waiting list? Am I optimistic to think I could get into the University of Michigan Law School in the first place?*

"I just hope you don't lose your passion and optimism when school begins. Or when you enter the real world."

*Yup.*

"This was great," she said at the end of our meal. "I wish all my breakfasts were this fun. I know you'll find success wherever you end up."

If that sounds like a polite reassurance to you, you're not a lawyer. If you were, you'd see it for what it was: a disclaimer.

My parents and I flew to Las Vegas to tour the UNLV law school. It was 113 degrees, and I couldn't even make it from the main lecture hall to the library.[22] UNLV might have the best law school in the country, but if I can't walk from a school's lecture hall to its library without catching fire, it's not for me.

Instead of touring the campus, I spent the evening in the Bellagio poker room learning that beating my buddy Steve the law clerk in our weekly heads-up game didn't mean I could beat a group of eighty-year-old retirees who spent nine hours a day supplementing their Social Security checks with the money of (the parents of) Phil Ivey wannabes like me.

Back home, another #10 envelope from the University of

---

[22] My parents made the walk and reported that they could see the Bellagio hotel from the law library's windows. How's that for a distraction?

Michigan awaited me in the mailbox. My mom took the rejection harder than I did, so I was put in the odd position of having to console her, wiping away the tears she was shedding on my behalf. This was a brilliant mothering strategy on her part; by forcing me to console her, she distracted me from my own sadness and disappointment. Later in the day the rejection hit me.

My dad wanted me to continue his law school legacy more than anything in the world, but he couldn't really complain about paying $18,000 less per year for DePaul. So we flew to Chicago.

The DePaul University College of Law is located in Chicago's business district, the Loop. The Loop is home to the Sears Tower and the Art Institute of Chicago (see *Ferris Bueller's Day Off*), the Daley Center (see *The Blues Brothers*), the Daley Plaza (see *The Fugitive*), Buckingham Fountain (see *Married with Children*), and all the other major midwestern landmarks that aren't in New York. (Aside from the St. Louis Gateway Arch and . . . did I mention the Arch?)

My mom booked us a hotel right on Michigan Avenue, the street on which the Hancock Building, the Water Tower Place mall, the Magnificent Mile shopping stretch, Millennium Park, and the Art Institute are all located. We fought our way through a stampede of tourists from the hotel to the Lewis Center, the law school's main building. DePaul Law administrators brag that the Lewis Center is located right in the heart of downtown Chicago, which, while true, is really just a polite way of saying, "Watch out for the homeless guy urinating on the sidewalk behind you."[23]

The Dean of Admissions, a stocky game show host trapped in the life of a midwestern law school administrator, greeted my family and led us to the Lewis Center's sixth floor and through a pair of massive doors, which swung silently open into DePaul's mock courtroom.

The Dean of Admissions hit us with a barrage of DePaul University College of Law facts:

- The current mayor of Chicago, Richard M. Daley, graduated from DePaul, as did two former mayors.
- Over 250 judges graduated from DePaul as well.
- Though DePaul is a Catholic university, it has a faculty exchange program with the Hebrew University in Jerusalem.
- DePaul was the first law school in Illinois to admit Jews.

I couldn't help but feel the Dean of Admissions was looking at my parents and me as he spouted off those last two facts.

The one fact the dean didn't mention was the DePaul University College of Law's *U.S. News & World Report* ranking. The reason the Dean of Admissions didn't mention DePaul's ranking was that DePaul hadn't made the Top

[23] I saw this happen right outside the Lewis Center one afternoon.

100 list; DePaul was a Tier 3 School.[24] Nobody at DePaul, I soon learned, talked about the school's ranking. Sore subject.

The dean shook our hands vigorously and passed us off to a student named Alexis, a girl from South Carolina with pink sparkles on her cheeks and purple sparkles around her eyes. Alexis was so excited to show us around the school that it made everybody uncomfortable, except for Alexis herself, who was too excited to notice how uncomfortable the rest of us were. DePaul must have imported this girl from the drama department and given her a script with the following stage direction: "Don't be afraid to take this Law Student Tour Guide character over the top. However big you think this character should be played, play it bigger."

"So how *is* everybody? Can you believe you're *actually* here? *Actually* going to law school? This is so exciting!"

*Apparently.*

"Well, it looks like you guys—*and gals;* I see you back there, ladies—have already gone over the basics, so now I'm going to show you around the school and let you in on a few of the building's secrets."[25]

Alexis walked us to the law library explaining that every week first-year students attend "Thursday Night Bar Review" meetings. Then she pulled me and the other prospective students aside and told us that Thursday Night Bar Review had nothing to do with the bar exam and every-

[24] Fifty schools = 1 tier.

[25] For the record, Alexis never made good on this promise.

thing to do with patronizing new pubs and reviewing them.

My father asked me what Alexis had told us, but I was too embarrassed to say. One of the other prospective students must have snitched, though, because a parent asked, "Just how much drinking goes on here?"

Alexis gave us a look of disappointment. We had breached the sacred tour guide/prospective student code of confidentiality. Then she let the parents in on the Thursday Night Bar Review "joke."

I've never seen so many parents roll their eyes in unison.

We strode through the library's fourth floor.

"This is where you come to get *serious* work done," Alexis said. "The only trouble with studying here is the no food or drink policy, but," she whispered, "if you're real sneaky, you can probably bring a bottle of water and a small box of raisins in. And if somebody complains, just tell them Alexis said it was okay."

Alexis asked if we had any questions.

"Something is missing," my father said, and I feared he was going to mention a particular volume of a highly specialized tax publication or, worse, a specific issue of the *Michigan Law Review*.

"Students," he continued. "Didn't the Dean of Admissions tell us that finals are next week?"

"I think a lot of students are studying at home this weekend," Alexis said.

My father didn't buy it, but he wasn't about to embarrass me by pressing the matter further. He wasn't going to break into a story about how, when he was in school, he had to wait twenty minutes just to get a seat in the University of Michigan law library reading room.

My dad walked me through the University of Michigan law library when I was ten, and the experience ruined me for all other law libraries. People say that the University of Michigan law library looks like a movie set, but saying that doesn't do the building justice, which is doubly unfortunate, as justice is the very thing about which people go there to learn.

The building's gigantic archways, exquisite stained-glass windows, and imposing chandeliers are said to inspire even the most reluctant students to crack their books. Walking through the reading room, students feel a profound connection to the great Michigan lawyers of the past—they do until somebody's cell phone goes off with its ringer tone set to Jay-Z's "Money, Cash, Hoes."

The Gothic architectural period ended in the sixteenth century, but Thomas Edison didn't invent the first practical lightbulb until 1879, so, in the name of authenticity, the University of Michigan's law library's courtyard was built with no artificial lighting whatsoever, which explains why John Norman "Co-ed Killer" Collins—whom one of my father's friends would go on to defend—hung out there.

Originally, in response to the murders, the University of Michigan installed street lamps. The law students thought the street lamps destroyed the courtyard's aesthetic integrity, so these future lawyers and politicians tore the lamps down with their bare hands.

My father was one of the diggers.

You'd think he would have been more receptive to electric lighting given what happened one night in the fall of 1968. My mother was sitting on the steps that lead from the law library courtyard to the reading room, waiting for him to finish studying, when a man approached and offered to walk her to her car. My mom, who had seen a police sketch artist's rendering of John Norman Collins, noticed a resemblance. She screamed, ran to her car, drove to her apartment, and called the police.

When Collins was arrested in 1969, my mom saw his photograph in the paper. It was the same guy.

I wonder how she felt about my dad tearing down the street lamps.

The DePaul University College of Law library looks comparatively bland and has no checkered romantic past. The only checkered part is the bathroom floor.

Alexis walked us through the computer center, the student lounge, and a few classrooms—all beige. After the tour concluded, my parents and I joined the tourist stampede, following it up Michigan Avenue to the Water Tower Place mall food court. In the evening, we took a taxi to Lincoln Park and attended our family friend Hanna's one-woman show about how the guys she dates are either not Jewish enough or way too Jewish,[26] and how her dreams to write for *Saturday Night Live* haven't yet been realized.

She'll be in law school within four years.

---

[26] Like Josh, who prayed every time he and Hanna hooked up, and Aaron, who begged Hanna to study Torah with him and dreamed of becoming a Rabbi. Aaron, Hanna tells me, is now an atheist . . . and a law student.

I spent the next two months back in Michigan, where my days as a cowbellist were coming to an end. During my final "Banana Man" performance, I thought about how large the maturity gap between me and the Tally Hall guys was about to grow: the following month, they were driving to New Jersey to sing songs about bananas, rapping robots,[27] and the Olsen twins;[28] I was driving to Chicago to become a lawyer.

[27] *We're stereosonic. We're animatronic.*
*We're rapping with the robo-electronic Ebonics.*

[28] *Mary-Kate and Ashley, I hope you understand*
*That I love you a lot and I want to be your man,*
*And I think that it'd be totally cool*
*If I hung around in your apartment and enrolled in your school.*

# Chapter Two

## Spotting the Brownnoser

DePaul's admissions brochure features a "Where to Live" guide suggesting apartments in the Gold Coast area ("the Gold Coast boasts beaches, lakefront biking, and jogging"), Wrigleyville ("Home to Wrigley Field and the world-famous Chicago Cubs, this tree-lined neighborhood sports classic brownstones, courtyard apartments . . ."), and Lincoln Park ("Most DePaul students live in this north side enclave, which surrounds DePaul's main campus and includes its library, computer labs, and sports facilities"). The one place the brochure does not recommend is the Loop, because living in the Loop would be like living in Times Square, only with fewer billboards.

A few days before my parents and I returned to Chicago to find an apartment, DePaul sent out academic schedules. Second- and third-year students select which classes they want and when they want to take them; first-year students have no say in either matter. My schedule informed me that I was in Section 2, with classes beginning at nine o'clock (!) in the morning on Mondays, Wednesdays, and Fridays and 9:30 A.M. on Tuesdays and Thursdays. By contrast, during the later half of college I did everything I could to avoid taking classes that began before one.

Thus, my apartment hunt had a single objective: a place that would minimize my morning commute. That objective led me to the thirty-eight-story Frontier Plaza building on Michigan Avenue, directly between the Magnificent Mile shopping stretch and Millennium Park. The Frontier Plaza building was just seven blocks from the Lewis Center, so I could make the door-to-door walk in fifteen minutes.[29] Frontier Plaza also has a glass-domed swimming pool on the thirty-eighth floor, which is to say, it was way out of my (parents') price range.

"Yes, the building is beautiful," my dad said. "No, you can't live here."

I did what any future lawyer would do: I made my case.

"I know this place is expensive," I began, "but living here with the scholarship would still cost much less than living somewhere else without the scholarship. Plus, if I live close to the school, I won't have to worry about the L stalling or the bus getting caught in traffic; I can walk to school every day. I'll have no excuses for missing class or even being late."

My parents went for it. Of course, underlying their willingness to let me live there was an unspoken agreement: my parents would pay my obscene rent, and I would get a high-paying lawyer job and use the money (left over after paying

[29] That's a fantastic commute by almost anybody's standards, but not my father's. When he went to law school, he lived in the law quad all three years. He says that he could get from his room to his classroom in thirty seconds flat.

for my trophy wife's feng shui consultant) to buy them a Floridian retirement villa equipped with solid gold bathtub grab bars.

The following week, my parents helped move my stuff to Chicago, and before they left, I had my dad tie every one of my ties so I could slip them on and off as needed.

"You should set an academic goal for yourself," my father said.

"Not failing?"

"You can do better than that."

"I was joking."

"How about holding on to your scholarship," my mother suggested.

"That sounds reasonable," my father said.

"I only need a three point three to keep my scholarship. Maybe I should aim higher?"

"I hope you do get something higher," said my dad, "but I think law school is going to be harder than you think."

If law school was half as tough as my father said it would be, I'd need a gym to work off all the stress. So I set out to find one. A modest quest, yes, but one that I undertook on my own; my parents had returned to Michigan and left me alone in the city I'd call home for the next three years.

I passed hundreds of tourists, dozens of homeless Chicagoans, and handfuls of street performers, including a silver robo-man dancing to Michael Jackson classics. The tourists preferred him to the balloon-making angel on the unicycle by a ratio of 4:1, even though (1) he reeked of dirt and paint and (2) he was dancing to the music of a forty-five-year-old slumber-party organizer.

The tourists liked the guy manipulating three marionettes at once but not the woman wearing the Victorian dress and waving, nor the girl playing the accordion next to a "Squeezing for Schooling" sign. I was also pleased to see that the tourists liked the caped Millennium Park street magician; if law school didn't work out, I now knew I could find alternative employment close by.

I struck up a conversation with the magician, who told me that the number-one rule of street performing is "Nothing attracts a crowd like a crowd" and the number two rule of street performing is "When you're bombing, just end the show—it's not like anybody paid for a ticket." I stored the lessons in my memory bank. Then the magician told me that there was a Second City Health Club just four blocks away.

The Second City Health Club in Chicago's business district is for serious athletes only; you have to walk down six lengths of stairs just to reach the locker rooms. By the time you start your cardio, you're already out of breath. Also notable: the gym pays a septuagenarian security guard to sit in the men's locker room and, as far as I could tell, watch men change. I'll put modesty aside for a moment and say that, back in Michigan, I was the Arnold Schwarzenegger of my parents' gym. The other gym members were mostly seventy-year-old

Jewish grandparents . . . but the point is, if push came to shove, I could have taken any one of them. In comparison, I was the Second City Health Club's Arnold Horshack.[30]

To compensate for my feelings of inferiority during my first Chicago workout, I lifted weights much heavier than I should have. Afterward, the only thing that hurt more than my quadriceps was my ego. The women at the Second City Health Club were attractive and employed. Back in college, I might charm girls with my virtuoso cowbell playing or with exaggerated tales of my virtuoso cowbell playing. The women at the Chicago gym, by comparison, wanted mature, financially secure men. They didn't want to date law students, and they certainly didn't want to date cowbell-playing magicians. They didn't want to date anybody whose best pickup line was "I don't live with my parents anymore."

Walking home, I passed by the caped Millennium Park magician again and snuck a peek in his top hat. Despite the big crowds, he had made only a handful of change in the ninety minutes since I had last seen him.

*If I'm ever going to stand a chance with a Second City Health Club woman, this law school thing had better work out.*

The neoclassical 756,000-square-foot Harold Washington public library has three five-story windows and over seventy miles of bookshelves. Before riding the escalator to

---

[30] Of TV's *Welcome Back, Kotter.* I had insomnia and watched a lot of *Nick-at-Nite* as an adolescent.

the basement, I took in the mosaic mural that depicts the life of Harold Washington, Chicago's first black mayor. Each stage of the mayor's life is represented by a page of a book. The books are spread haphazardly across Washington's desk, and they form a mountain, which represents Washington's mayoral electoral victory.

I hadn't gone to the library to read; I'd gone to meet my classmates and professors at orientation.

The girl behind the check-in table looked up.

"You must be Rick."

The girl pointed to a plastic shoe box containing two pin-on name tags, one of which was mine.

"Unless you're Adrienne . . . ," she continued.

I had arrived fifteen minutes before the introductory speeches were set to begin, and out of 240 students in the incoming class I was second to last to show up. I took a seat next to a guy wearing a dress shirt, sweater-vest, and Yankees baseball cap perched on a nest of blond hair. His name was Erik. The name tag pinned to his thigh told me so.

"Where you from, Rick?"

"Have you seen the movie 8 *Mile*?"

"You're from there?"

"I am."

Close enough. Gave me some edge.

Erik told me he had just graduated from the University of Iowa, where he was the president of his fraternity. Before I could ask him about all the awful things he did to humiliate pledges,[31] the Dean of Admissions asked for our attention and then started his speech.

"Welcome to the DePaul University College of Law," he said. "It's good to see so many familiar faces in the audience. Now, I'm not going to give you the 'look to your left, look to your right' speech, even though I know you're all expecting it."

The Dean of Admissions was way off on that one, as indicated by all the blank stares; we were neither expecting nor familiar with the "look to your left" speech.

"You don't know what I'm talking about?" the Dean of Admissions asked. "What year were you born?"

We were mostly born in the early eighties; *The Paper Chase,* which popularized the "look to your left" speech, came out in 1973.[32]

The Dean of Admissions turned things over to the Dean of Internal Affairs, an Asian woman in her early thirties,

---

[31] A college friend of mine rushed one of the University of Michigan's predominantly Jewish fraternities. He was made to strip naked and watch homosexual pornography along with his fellow pledges. Then he was told to jump from the second story of his frat house into a pile of leaves.

[32] The speech goes like this: "Look to your left. Look to your right. One of the people you just looked at won't be graduating three years from now." Law schools used to give this speech regularly. One of my former Barnes & Noble "coworkers," who graduated from Wayne State University Law School, told me even he remembered getting the "look to your left" speech back in '57.

Law schools just don't fail students like they used to. They need the tuition dollars to stay competitive.

whose job, unlike that of the previous dean, did not require a cheerful demeanor. Rather, her job was to scare the hell out of us with horror stories about the Committee on Character and Fitness:

"Two years ago there was a student who was the first guy in his family to go to college, and he racked up two UIPs—that stands for Urinating In Public, by the way—and the Committee on Character and Fitness said he couldn't practice law in the state of Illinois for two years. He came crying to me, but there was nothing I could do for him."

Silence.

"Four years ago there was a student who got As and some Bs. She hopped a Red Line turnstile, once, got caught, and didn't tell the Committee on Character and Fitness about it. Naturally, they found out, so she couldn't become a lawyer. She came crying to me, but there was nothing I could do for her."

More silence.

"Have you ever broken the law? Did you get caught? Have you violated a court order? Do you have a drug problem? If so, we need to talk."

I've only been to prison twice: once when I toured the Jackson County facility with my Cub Scout troop, and once when I visited Alcatraz with my parents. The only time I found myself on the wrong side of the law was in 1998. Driving home from an a cappella concert in Ann Arbor, I took the wrong exit and got caught in a notorious speed trap. I wasn't watching my speedometer because I was rocking out to *Primer,* a limited-edition Rockapella[33] CD.[34] I considered bringing this to the dean's attention but decided against it.

The Dean of Internal Affairs continued, "If you've already done something that you think might disqualify you from becoming an attorney in the state of Illinois, then come and talk to me next week, because there's no point in going through the next three years if you can't be a lawyer at the end of it."

Erik's face had gone white.

Criminal law professor Robert Barry, a forty-something graduate of the University of Texas School of Law and former Knox County State's Attorney, stepped up to the podium wielding a Louisville Slugger, which he swung several times during the course of his welcoming introduction. He said that he brought the bat in as an example of *demonstrative evidence.*[35] He probably meant to say the bat was *real evidence,*[36] but it's best not to correct a six-foot-four former Knox County State's Attorney swinging a baseball bat around.

Barry said that he would see some of us in class on Monday. He was talking about those of us in Section 2.

[33] Whom you might remember as the house "band" from *Where in the World Is Carmen Sandiego?*

[34] To the member of the Committee on Character and Fitness assigned to read this book: if loving a cappella music is a crime, then find me guilty.

[35] *Demonstrative evidence:* evidence in the form of representation of an object. Common examples of demonstrative evidence include maps, charts, photographs, videotapes, and scale models.

[36] *Real evidence:* evidence that was actually involved in the facts of a case.

Head Dean Glen Weissenberger spoke last: "You've heard a lot about us, the faculty, and you've heard a lot about DePaul, but now I'd like to talk to you about something else: you. All two hundred and forty of you. Some of you came here from state college; some of you came here from Harvard.[37] One of you has a Ph.D. in organic chemistry, another of you has one in materials engineering. One of you even designed spacecraft parts for Boeing.

"One of you is the president of a gospel choir. One taught English in Ghana. One survived testicular cancer. One lost over one hundred pounds in two years. One was attacked by sharks. One worked for NATO in Kosovo as a counterintelligence agent with the U.S. Army.

"One of you is a professional magician, and that particularly excites me because I used to be a professional magician, too."

Everybody laughed and looked through the crowd, presumably to see who the magician was, as if I would wear my top hat and cape to orientation.

Afterward, I tracked the Head Dean down.

"So you're the magician?"

"Been doing it my whole life."

"Same here," said the dean. "Children's parties?"

"A few dozen."

"That's nothing. I've done hundreds."

[37] The Harvard kid dropped out during the second week of the second semester.

We went back and forth like that for ten minutes, comparing notes on *double-lifts*,[38] thumb palms, and slipknots, not noticing the crowd of students gathering around us. When I finally looked up and realized I had been monopolizing the guy everybody was waiting to meet, I politely ended our conversation.

But the students gravitated toward me, not the Head Dean; a nervous girl wearing an ankle-length skirt and a crucifix necklace with matching bracelet spoke on the group's behalf:

"What were you two talking about?"

"The dean offered to set me up with Kirkland and Ellis," I said, smugly. "Said he liked the cut of my jib." The students looked at me with dismay and no small amount of terror.

"I'm kidding," I said, "I'm the magician. We talked about magic."

"Oh," replied the girl, whose name was Cassandra. The group dissipated, except for one guy with curly hair wearing a black T-shirt and black jeans. His tag read "Marty."

"I thought *I* was the magician."

I had made my first law school friend, and he could tie five different slipknots.

"It's funny you mentioned Kirkland and Ellis," Marty said, "because Ellis is my uncle. We're having lunch together tomorrow. Did you actually want to meet him?"

---

[38] *Double-lift:* two cards displayed as one.

"Uh, *yes*."

"Twelve fifteen. Luxbar. You're welcome to join us. He'll pay, so don't worry about that."

"This sounds too good to be true."

"It is. I'm totally messing with you right now. I'm pretty sure Ellis died a long time ago. Do you still want to grab lunch, though?"

"Sure."

There was a ninety-minute introductory Legal Writing class scheduled immediately following the introductory comments.

Professor Devenpeck, a sixty-year-old nearly bald man, entered Room 1001 frowning and carrying two mugs: one filled with coffee, the other empty. Devenpeck was a visiting professor who had grown up near my hometown.

"I don't know about any of you, but I had to be here at six forty-five this morning."

Not concerning oneself with social pleasantries is one of the perks that comes with being a visiting professor.

"Let's get going so we're not backed up by next week."

That was it by way of introduction. Professor Devenpeck started talking and didn't stop—not even for the Brown Line L trains, which screamed past the classroom every ten minutes—until one hour and thirty minutes later.

Because school hadn't officially started, I wasn't expecting a substantive introductory class, so I hadn't brought my laptop. Instead, I took notes by hand, which was problematic because I can't really read my own handwriting.[39] I suppose I've used up all of my manual dexterity on card tricks. But even if I could have read my own writing, my notes would have been useless, because I couldn't understand 90 percent of what Devenbeck was saying.

I'm pretty sure he was talking about the different things that go into judges' case opinions, but that was all I could make out for sure. Devenpeck wrongly assumed that we already knew a wide array of legal terms and concepts, and his introductory lesson depended on our knowing them. Also, because there were no pauses in his speech, none of us had the chance to raise our hand and ask, "What does *'certiorari'*[40] mean?" or, even better, "Could you repeat everything you said over the past ninety minutes, only this time in English?"

At the end of class, Devenpeck passed out a *wrongful death*[41] case about a man who crashed his golf cart into an oak tree,

---

[39] When I was in fifth grade, my mom took me to the William Beaumont Hospital Center for Human Development to see if I had a learning disability. My single area of "Marked Concern," according to the Interdisciplinary Staffing Summary Conference Synopsis, was "pencil control and graphomotor skills." I had "a very maladaptive, almost whole-fisted pencil grip with marked increased pressure. Indeed, [I] broke the whole bottom half off of the first pencil that [I] used because of this pressure."

[40] *Certiorari:* The present passive infinitive of the Latin verb *certiorare,* which is a contraction of *certiorem facere,* which means to make certain. Sorry, Devenpeck. I should have assumed.

[41] *Wrongful death:* A civil action brought by the close relatives of the deceased. A civil action, by the way, differs from a criminal case as
*(continued next page)*

and told us to "brief the case" by separating and summarizing the opinion's facts, *issues, dicta,* and *holding.*[42]

We thought we were in the clear, but then somebody's cell phone went off.

"I'll ignore that this one time," Devenpeck announced. "So you're welcome. From now on, if somebody's phone goes off during my class, its owner will be asked to leave."

With that, Devenpeck left the room.

Adrienne, the girl who had arrived at orientation after me, said, "Did any of that make sense to any of you?"

We all stayed an extra five minutes, bonding over our mutual confusion.

That evening there was a meet and greet in the courtyard of the University Center dorm, where first-year law students from three different law schools lived. We were encouraged to drink as much free beer and wine as we wanted, but I didn't because I figured the alcohol offer could be a test—a clever way of weeding out the alcoholics before classes began. I was wrong: after a student named Bruce fell into a bush, he was encouraged to cut to the front of the open bar line and replenish his drink.

––––––––––––––––––

follows: in a criminal case, the government seeks to put somebody who broke a criminal law in prison; in a civil case, a private party sues another private party for damages (i.e., money, usually) and, unless one of the parties is held in contempt of court (e.g., *I'm* out of order? *You're* out of order! This whole court is out of order!"), nobody goes to jail.

[42] *Issues:* Questions of law; *dicta:* nonbinding statements; *holding:* the court's legal decision.

I spotted Erik carrying a cup of beer in his left hand and a glass of red wine in his right. He was telling a group of three girls that he liked red wine but didn't want to stain his teeth, so after every sip of red, he'd rinse with beer.

"It's a trick I invented back in undergrad," he explained.

*What a charmer.*

Erik was making a lot of friends, but so was I. I took names, got stories, tore and restored a few cocktail napkins, and even scored two phone numbers, including Adrienne's. One phone number I didn't get was Cassandra's, the girl with the crucifix necklace. Cassandra was exactly the type of girl who would never date a guy like me, and naturally that turned me on.

"Did you see the guy who fell in the bush?" I asked.

"I heard about it," Cassandra replied.

"No bush falling for you."

I indicated Cassandra's empty hand. She was the only person in sight without a drink.

"Would you like to wait in line with me to get a drink?" I offered.

"Oh, I don't drink," Cassandra said.

"How about some food?" I continued, undaunted.

Cassandra agreed, and we took what remained from the appetizer table: some radishes, yellow squash sticks, and leftover meatball pieces. Then an Asian girl wearing a power suit and carrying herself like a girl wearing a power suit approached Cassandra and me.

"Hi! I'm Kimberly Mitsuya."

She shook my hand with both of hers.

"You've got my vote," I told her.

"I don't get it."

"Only politicians shake hands like that."

"Guess I'm the exception," she said.[43]

As I noshed on a meatblob, Kimberly walked Cassandra and me through the highlights of her curriculum vitae, which included working as some congressman's intern. After a few minutes, I pulled the two nearest people into our group, hoping to mix the conversation up. Thankfully, Nadeeka, a large Sri Lankan girl, and Dan, a lanky guy in Buddy Holly glasses, broke the rule forbidding immediately changing the topic of a conversation you've just joined. In doing so, they also broke the one about discussing politics and/or race with people you've just met:

"I feel like the only nonwhite person here," Nadeeka said, despite the dozens of nonwhites, including Kimberly, standing all around us.

Dan, who was white, concurred: "I know."

Dan told me that he and Nadeeka had met during their Legal Writing class and that they were both planning to go into public interest law and work in third-world countries.

"I just can't stop thinking about how half the people in the world are impoverished," Nadeeka said.

"It is sad," I said. "The number is way less than half, though."

Nadeeka snapped, "*I* studied international relations at

---

[43] A week later I'd find out she wasn't.

Georgetown—my mother is a Regent there—and I wrote a fifty-page paper on the topic, so I'm pretty sure *I* know what I'm talking about. What did *you* do in college?"

Nadeeka glared at me.

"Played the cowbell, dressed up in gorilla costumes, chicken costumes. That kind of thing."

"So why are you even here?"

At that point, Erik butted into the conversation and invited me to the bar. Then he gave Cassandra a shameless once-over—visibly upsetting Nadeeka, who had been given a zero-over—and welcomed her to join us.

"As I was just telling Rick here, I don't drink."

Erik tugged on Cassandra's necklace and said, "Because of Jesus?"

She pushed his hand away.

"You *obviously* wouldn't understand." Then she walked away.

I was glad Cassandra had rejected Erik's offer. If Cassandra was going to go for any guy who wasn't her type, I decided, that guy who wasn't her type was going to be me.

After Erik followed Cassandra away, hopefully to apologize, Nadeeka asked me, "Are you actually going to hang out with that asshole?"

"Do you know him?" I asked.

"I know his type."

Erik had assembled a group of eight students, Adrienne included, by the elevator. Having gone to high school for four years, I easily recognized this group as the cool kids. Apparently none of them recognized that I wasn't one of them.

We took taxis to McFadden's, a Gold Coast bar that combines the charm of a frat house with the aroma of a Bowery flophouse. We drank Long Island Iced Teas and Jack and Cokes as Adrienne flirted with Erik and me equally. It was frustrating. Three or four drinks into the evening, Adrienne announced, "It's time to start drinking *for real* now."

"Real" drinking entailed shots and shooters.

The biggest difference between the cool kids like Erik and Adrienne and the serious kids like Dan and Nadeeka wasn't their alcohol tolerance; it was their motivation for becoming lawyers: the cool kids didn't want to go into public interest law; they wanted to use their J.D.'s to make large amounts of money, and after six drinks, they weren't afraid to admit it.

Seven drinks into the night, Erik and Adrienne stood up to dance. I was about to follow when I noticed Adrienne's credit card on the table. I picked it up and ran after her. But after five minutes, I couldn't find anybody from DePaul. After ten minutes, the alcohol, smoke, and noise got to me. I sent Adrienne a text message ("i have ur stuff. u left it at the table. where r u?"), but she didn't respond. So I left.

I called Adrienne the following day and heard Erik in the background, asking why somebody was calling so early.

It was one thirty.

The Dean of Internal Affairs told us to buy our casebooks at the Barnes & Noble on the bottom floor of the DePaul

Center, the building located just west of the Lewis Center. I needed books for Criminal Law with Professor Barry, Legal Writing with Professor Devenpeck, Constitutional Law with Professor Laurel, Contract Law with Professor Dewey, and Civil Procedure (whatever that was) with Professor Ryder. I decided to buy books for my second-semester Property and Tort classes while I was at it.

I asked a store worker to direct me to the law books.

"Need help carrying everything?" she asked.

She couldn't have weighed more than a hundred pounds; I laughed politely and declined.

My first-year books cost just under two thousand dollars and stood over thirty inches tall. I felt a bit foolish for turning down the offered help. I left my books with the clerk, found a nearby luggage shop, bought a rolling bag, and returned. I filled my backpack, my rolling bag, and three shopping bags with the books and lugged them to the bookstore café to meet up with Erik—he hadn't changed out of his dress shirt and sweater-vest—so I could give him Adrienne's credit card. I also had to study for Con Law.

Professor Laurel had told us via e-mail to read *Marbury v. Madison* before our first class. I imagined his lecture would go like this: Professor Laurel would walk to the front of the room, set his class roster on the podium, and say, "Welcome to Constitutional Law. Now, Mr. Lax, in *Marbury v. Madison,* what did Chief Justice John Marshall mean when he said: 'Affirmative words are often, in their operation, negative of other objects than those affirmed; and in this case, a negative or exclusive sense must be given to them or they have no operation at all'?"[44]

This paranoia stemmed from Professor Laurel's class syllabus, which read: "Students will not be graded on class participation, except that if a student is absent or unprepared when called on for class discussion, his or her grade will be lowered one level."

I spent an hour reading the eight-page *Marbury v. Madison* opinion, and having done so, I couldn't for the life of me say what the case was about. I read through the opinion a second time, taking notes in the margins. On my third reading, my notes from round two proved useless, consisting as they did of one-word questions (e.g., "Why?" or "Huh?") and acronymous rhetorical questions (e.g., "WTF?"). I spent my third reading wondering what was going through my mind during the second.

After the fourth, miraculously, things began to make sense.

On his last day in office, President Adams appointed William Marbury justice of the peace for the District of Columbia. Marbury's commission was signed and stamped, but not delivered on time. Incoming President Thomas Jefferson's Secretary of State, James Madison, refused to deliver

---

[44] That sentencelike gathering of words and punctuation is a real quote from Marshall's *Marbury* opinion. I can't decide if it's a truism, a contradiction, or a joke that the Chief Justice threw in to scare first-year law students for generations to come.

the commission. Marbury asked the Supreme Court to issue a *writ of mandamus*[45] forcing Madison to deliver the commission, claiming that the Judiciary Act gave it the power to do this sort of thing, even though the Constitution forbade such writs.

The real issue was this: could the Supreme Court strike down legislation like the Judiciary Act that it found "repugnant to" the Constitution?

The answer seems obvious—especially when I use the word "repugnant" (as Marshall did in the *Marbury* opinion). But in 1803 things weren't so clear. The Constitution doesn't explicitly give the Judicial Branch the authority to rule on acts of Congress.

In other words, the Supreme Court had to rule on whether it had the power to determine which acts of Congress were repugnant to the Constitution before it could rule on which acts of Congress were repugnant to the Constitution. The Court ruled in favor of the former and then ruled that the Constitution did indeed trump the Judiciary Act.

Thus, they refused Marbury his writ.[46]

---

[45] *Writ of mandamus:* a court order to a government official (or lower court).

[46]

If you had to read that just once to understand it, that's because I wrote it in the English language. Chief Justice John Marshall wrote his judicial opinions in Greek, which Justice Moore translated into Latin, which Justice Paterson translated into English.

That's a little theory of mine. I have only *circumstantial evidence*[47] to back it up. Why else would the opinion read, "Impressions are often received without much reflection or examination, and it is not wonderful, that in such a case as this, the assertion, by an individual, of his legal claims in a court of justice, to which claims it is the duty of that court to attend, should at first view be considered by some, as an attempt to intrude into the cabinet, and to intermeddle with the prerogatives of the executive," when it could read: "It's sad that people look at this as an attempt to violate the separation of powers"?

Someone needed to sit Marshall down and tell him, "Johnny, you're the Chief Justice of the Supreme Court of the United States of America. You don't have to impress us anymore; *we accept you.*"

I spent three hours reading constitutional law and two more reading contract law. By the time I'd finished, it was dark outside. Packing up, I noticed student tour guide Alexis sitting at a table across the café with her head buried in a Business Organization casebook, her posture grotesque, her face red and puffy.

When questioning a witness on a prior inconsistent

[47] *Circumstantial evidence:* Facts that indirectly suggest a conclusion.

statement, the trial lawyer is tempted to ask, "Were you lying then or are you lying now?" (Good lawyers don't ask this question because it gives opposing witnesses the opportunity to explain away their contradictions.) I wanted to ask Alexis, "Which is the real you? The bubbly DePaul fanatic leading the school tour or the frazzled hunchback I see today?" But there was no need to ask: this was clearly the real Alexis.

The morning of my first class, I somehow woke up before eight and tried to read *Marbury* one last time. Halfway through, I caught myself reciting sentences by memory; I'd hit the point of diminishing returns, so I slipped on a pre-tied tie, loaded up my rolling bag, and went to class.

I took the Lewis Center elevator to Room 815, a beige lecture hall with curved walls, a low ceiling, and no windows. The DePaul University College of Law faculty, I assume, felt that a bit of claustrophobia is a small price to pay for classroom suicide prevention. All of my classes, except for Legal Writing, would be held in Room 815.

I arrived ten minutes early, but, once again, I wasn't early enough: the only open seats were those in the front and back rows. Dan and Nadeeka sat in the second-to-front row; Erik sat in the back; Adrienne sat directly in front of Erik; Cassandra and Marty sat in the middle. I was forced to take a seat at the far end of the back row, the absolute farthest seat from the podium. I vowed to show up earlier to my next class.

There's an old poker saying: if you look around the table and you can't spot the sucker, you're him. The same can be said of law school: if you look around the classroom and you can't spot the brownnoser, you're him.

By the end of Laurel's first Con Law class, I couldn't spot the brownnoser.

Professor Laurel strutted into the classroom wearing matching argyle suspenders and socks.[48] He welcomed us to Constitutional Law, but he didn't call on me as I had feared. Instead, he asked for a volunteer.

The room went quiet, and stayed that way. Laurel smiled and tugged the lapels of his tweed sport coat, seemingly pleased by the silent tension. Ten or fifteen seconds in, I realized that I had never been nor, in all probability, would I ever again be so prepared for a class. The silence pressing in on me, I theorized that volunteering might prevent future Socratic victimization. I raised my hand.

"Yes. Your name?"

"Rick."

"Your surname?"

"Lax."

"Mr. Lax, please tell us about the political climate of the country at the time of *Marbury v. Madison.*"

"The political climate?"

Not the commanding intro for which I'd hoped. Repeating a question is a classic stall tactic, but I couldn't help it:

[48] I know what Laurel's socks looked like because Laurel had the habit of planting his feet, one at a time, on the first-row table, pulling up his pant legs, and then adjusting his socks, exposing what can only be described as an obscene amount of ankle.

*the political climate?* A total curveball! That stuff wasn't in the case. Luckily, I'd spent my freshman year at James Madison Residential College at MSU, so I knew a thing or two about James Madison.[49]

"An election, Mr. Lax? Was there an election going on at this time?"

"Yes."

"And who was running in this election?"

"John Adams and the Federalists were running against Thomas Jefferson and the Jeffersonian Republicans."

"How did it go?"

"Good—for Jefferson."

"And . . . ?"

And then I launched into the case. I said that the Federalist Congress passed the Judiciary Act, which created sixteen new Federal Circuit Court judgeships and a bunch of Justice of the Peace positions. That on his last day of office Adams nominated Federalist judges for all the positions. That the judges were confirmed by the lame-duck Federalist Congress. The words—many of them Marshall's—poured out of me. Also, I'm pretty sure I said "nevertheless" at some point.

A minute later, I ran out of facts. Either I had proven myself or Laurel was sick of hearing me talk, because he asked for another volunteer to give him the case's issues and holding. Because I had broken the volunteer barrier, students'

[49] Quite literally.

hands shot up left and right. They were eager to say things like "Jeffersonian Republicans" and "nevertheless," to bask in the residue of my polysyllabic glory.

That's the way I saw it, at least. I expected that after the lecture my classmates would hoist me on their shoulders and sing my praises. In reality, after the lecture my classmates didn't even make eye contact with me, let alone congratulate me. I got a "Nice work" from my friend Marty, but I think he was just being polite.

We had an hour-long break before Contract Law with Professor Dewey. I arrived back at Room 815 twenty minutes before class began. Though most people had camped out in their seats for the duration of the break, I found a seat next to Marty. Dewey, an African-American woman wearing a brown, ivory, and gold dress that wouldn't have looked out of place on a red carpet, entered and delivered the uplifting introduction we'd all been waiting for. When she said, "To this day, I find contract law fascinating," we believed her. Dewey told us we'd all do fine as long as we didn't fall behind on our readings.

"And if you do fall behind," she continued, "in this class or in any other, just come and see me and we'll get you back on track. And even if you don't have any problems, stop by my office to say hi. If you have the time, I recommend doing that with all your professors. It's always nice for us to put a face with a name. I have a seating chart"— Dewey held it up—"and, as you can see, it's blank. I'm going to pass it around the room, and when you get it fill your name in the box that corresponds to the seat you're sitting in. You can find your seat number on the back of your chair."[50]

Dewey passed the chart around, and then she taught us the fundamental rule of contract making: *bargained-for consideration:* "Promises," she explained, "are only enforceable if the promisor receives a benefit from the promisee in consideration of the promise." Dewey reviewed two cases that carved out exceptions to the bargained-for consideration rule. In the first, *Hamer v. Sidway,* William Story's uncle, William Story, Sr., promised his nephew $5,000 if he refrained from drinking, smoking, and gambling until his twenty-first birthday. Story the nephew kept his part of the deal but Story the uncle died before Story the nephew could collect. Sidway, the uncle's executor, then refused to give the $5,000 to Hamer, somebody to whom Story the nephew had promised the $5,000.

"This is a situation," Dewey explained, "devoid of bargained-for consideration. The uncle didn't really benefit from his nephew's abstinence—did he? Yet there's something unfair about Sidway not paying Hamer the money—right?"

---

[50] FIRST-YEAR TIP: Most professors employ do-it-yourself seating charts, and most professors call on each student only once per semester. If you want to be called on toward the beginning of the semester, write your name in large capital letters and use a felt-tip marker. If you want to be called on toward the end of the semester, write in cursive and use a dull pencil. If your last name is Smith, Jones, or Brown, you'll be called on during the first month of class no matter how illegibly you write. If your last name has four or more syllables, four or more consecutive consonants, an umlaut, or any sort of clicking sound, don't bother doing your reading until the last week of class, because you won't be called on until then.

In the second case, *Fienberg. v. Pfeiffer Co.*, a woman, Anna Sacks Fienberg, worked for the Pfeiffer Company for thirty-seven years and was promised a sizeable pension upon her retirement. Pfeiffer told Anna Fienberg that she could retire whenever she wanted, and Fienberg retired a year after the promise was made. But then Pfeiffer got new management, who cut off Fienberg's pension, claiming they were getting nothing in return. Therefore, Pfeiffer Co. argued, the promise to pay the pension was unenforceable.[51]

"Well," Dewey said, "the company is right: they weren't getting any real benefit from Fienberg's retirement. Still, it would be unfair to let the company deny her the money they had promised her—right?"

I had always assumed contract cases were won and lost on technicalities that bore no relationship to who "deserved" to win. But contract law, I saw, goes out of its way to help the deserving, the naïve, and the little guy—or, in this case, the little old lady. In *Hamer* the court held that a waiver of a legal right will substitute for consideration, and in *Fienberg* the court held that if you rely on a promise to your detriment, as Fienberg did, the promise becomes legally enforceable.

"In fact," Dewey concluded, "the Restatement of Contracts says a court can grant relief 'as justice requires,' which is a fancy way of saying 'whenever it's fair.'"

After class, Marty went to the library to study, and I went back to my apartment to not study. The not studying

---

[51] Usually pension plans are set up when employees start working, so the employees' continued employment counts as consideration.

didn't go well: I had a thirty-page Civ Pro reading to tackle, and I still didn't know what "civil procedure" was. The gaping hole in my understanding left me unable to enjoy *Iron Chef,* so I headed to the Barnes & Noble café to study.

Studying at home wasn't an option because when I'm in a room with a television, not watching it isn't an option.[52] Studying at the law library wasn't an option because almost all of my classmates studied there, and given the option of studying or complaining about studying, I'd do the latter. And given the option of studying or listening to me complain about studying, my classmates would do the latter because I'm such a fun complainer. Not to brag.

I started studying at bookstores during my freshman year at James Madison. Every evening around seven, I'd take my assigned reading to Shuler's Books on Grand River Avenue, which closed at ten. Walking from the entrance to the café, I'd grab a copy of the latest bestseller and read that until 9:45 P.M., at which point I'd leave, because the café workers didn't like it when customers stayed until closing. Doing this gave me the sensation of reading my assignment without the benefit of actually learning what I needed to know for class. Depending on your metaphoric preference, I was either killing zero birds with two stones or not eating the cake I didn't have.

Though I set out to study Civ Pro, I ended up studying the girl sitting at the table next to mine. Her name was

[52] Sorry, future wife!

April. She told me that she studied music at Juilliard, that she was spending the semester at her parents' house to care for her sick mother, and that she had just turned twenty-one. I was twenty-three, but April seemed mature for her age; she described herself as "a bit of a Francophile" and had just finished *I Am Charlotte Simmons,* the massive Tom Wolfe novel I had read the month before school began.

I asked April to watch my laptop while I ran to the bathroom.

"If it's stolen when I'm away," I said, "do you think you'd be legally responsible?"

"Yes?"

"Well, you're just saying that because you're not familiar with the doctrine of consideration."

"Stop. You're turning me on," April deadpanned.

"The doctrine of consideration says that for your promise to watch my stuff to be legally enforceable, I'd need to give you something in return."

This was a perfect opportunity to offer to buy April a drink, but I couldn't leave her with an incomplete understanding of the fundamental rule of contract making.

"According to the doctrine of promissory estoppel," I continued, "if I rely on your promise to my detriment—which I would be doing if I had you watch my stuff and it got stolen—it means that your promise to watch my stuff would be legally enforceable, even if I didn't give you anything in return."

When I returned from the bathroom—my laptop was

still there—I vanished and reproduced April's pinky ring.[53]

"That was like the best magic trick I've ever seen."

"What, no sarcastic remark? . . . Unless you were being sarcastic."

"I wasn't. Magic's more fun than law."

*Well, we're not going to go down that road.*

Finally, I asked April for that drink, because I knew I wouldn't be able to focus on my Civ Pro until I got a yes or a no. I got a no, but it came with a movie offer:

"We can sit in the front row and talk all the way through," she said.

"Deal," I replied, even though, legally, it wasn't.

Professor Ryder, a young adjunct professor, began Civ Pro class with *Tanner v. United States.* In it, Anthony Tanner was convicted of mail fraud, which, in the modern age, sounds harmless, if not downright charming (like whooping cough), but is actually a federal offense with a maximum penalty of twenty years.

Tanner appealed his guilty verdict to the Supreme Court, arguing that the lower United States Court of Appeals for the Eleventh Circuit wrongly refused to hear juror testimony about substance abuse going on in the jury room. Federal Rule of Evidence 606(b) allows jurors to testify about "outside influence."

[53] See Appendix A.

One juror told Tanner's lawyer that several of the jurors drank during lunch breaks and slept through the afternoons. Another juror said that he "felt like . . . the jury was on one big party," adding that he and other jurors "smoked marijuana quite regularly during the trial," that he "observed one juror ingest cocaine five times and another juror ingest cocaine two or three times," and that "one juror sold a quarter pound of marijuana to another juror during the trial, and took marijuana, cocaine, and drug paraphernalia into the courthouse."

Another juror described himself as "flying."

The Supreme Court upheld the guilty verdict: "However severe their effect and improper their use, drugs or alcohol voluntarily ingested by a juror seems no more an 'outside influence' than a virus, poorly prepared food, or a lack of sleep."

Professor Ryder asked for comments, and Erik had one: "In undergrad, I was in a fraternity, and there was a lot of . . . substance abuse going on in the house. Not from me, just the other guys . . ."

*Sure, Erik.*

". . . and these other guys always wanted to order pizza from Fusco's, which was pretty much the worst food on campus. Convincing them to order from Pizza House, which had great food—we're talking objectively great food—was hard enough when they were sober, but when they were high I couldn't convince them of anything because they couldn't even follow what I was saying."

"Thank you for sharing, Mr. . . . ?"

"Erik."

"Yes, thank you, Mr. Erik."

At the end of class, Ryder told us that she had assigned *Tanner* first "because it's a fun and easy case and I didn't want to scare any of you away."

"Next class," she continued, "we'll read *Pennoyer v. Neff* and begin our study of *jurisdiction*[54]—*in personam*, *in rem*, *quasi in rem*,[55] —and we won't stop for another two months. I can tell you right now: the first question on your exam will deal with jurisdiction, and it will be a long one. See you next time."

After a fifteen-minute break came Crim Law with Professor Barry, who didn't bring his baseball bat to class but did maintain the attitude of somebody wielding one:

"Your grade is based on a single three-hour exam given at the end of the semester," he said. "You say, 'That's unfair'? I say, when you're standing in front of a jury with a man's life on the line, you don't get a second chance—not if you're the prosecution—because of the *double-jeopardy rule*,[56] which I'm sure you're already familiar with from television."

Barry, I noticed, didn't move from behind the podium the entire lecture. He stood rigid, with impeccable posture, and spoke with a booming voice that made it clear I'd be getting no sleep in his class.

---

[54] *Jurisdiction:* the authority to administer justice.

[55] *In personam:* the jurisdiction granted to a court over people; *in rem:* the jurisdiction granted to a court over property; *quasi in rem:* the jurisdiction of a court based on a person's interest in property.

[56] *Double-jeopardy rule:* A criminal defendant can't be tried twice for the same crime.

"A single three-hour exam," Barry repeated. "No second chances here."

Barry explained the curve: 10 percent of us would get As, 20 percent would get B+'s, 30 percent would get Bs, 20 percent would get C+'s, and 20 percent of us would get Cs or worse. I had to stay at or above the twenty-fifth percentile to maintain a 3.3 average and keep my scholarship. Essentially, I had to outperform the person to my left, the person to my right, and the person to the right of the person to my right, who, I hoped, would be Erik.

Barry continued, "Let's get down to business: *mens rea.* Every crime has a *mens rea,* except for crimes that don't, but we'll go over those next time. *Mens rea* is Latin. It means 'guilty mind.' You're not guilty unless you have a guilty mind."

I don't speak Latin, but I felt pretty confident that Barry was butchering *mens rea.* But given how long Barry had been practicing and teaching law, I assumed the mispronunciation was deliberate, the way George W. Bush mispronounces "nuclear," because, well, he can.[57]

---

[57] In his book *Going Nucular: Language, Politics, and Culture in Confrontational Times,* linguist Geoffrey Nunberg writes: "In the mouths of [people like George W. Bush], 'nucular' is a choice, not an inadvertent mistake—a thinko, not a typo. I'm not sure exactly what they have in mind by it. Maybe it appeals to them to refer to the weapons in what seems like a folksy and familiar way, or maybe it's a question of asserting their authority—as if to say, "'We're the ones with our fingers on the button, and we'll pronounce the word however we damn well please.'"

"Turn to 5/4-3(a) of the Illinois Compiled Statutes: 'A person is not guilty of an offense unless he acts while having one of the criminal mental states.' Got it? Yes? Then let's look at an example of *mens rea*. Turn to page five fifty-one, section 11.02 of your textbook. Theft. Theft is a biggie in Chicago. Happens all the time—especially here in the downtown area."

Barry pointed his index finger toward the ceiling, and said, "Section 11.02 reads, and I quote, 'A person commits theft when he *knowingly* . . .' Stop right there. That's the *mens rea:* knowingly. In the great state of Illinois, the *mens rea* for the crime of theft is knowledge. If somebody accidentally drops his watch into your pocket and you see it happen and you walk away with it, you're a thief. It doesn't matter that you didn't intend to steal the watch; it matters that you knew you were doing it. Guilty!"

At that point, if Barry had been holding his bat, he would have banged it against the podium. Instead, he used his hand.

"Actions have consequences, people."

I dropped by Dewey's office to say hi as she had invited us all to do, but she wasn't there. The only professors in their offices were Devenpeck, whom I didn't want to talk to, and Barry, whom I was afraid to speak with. But I forced myself to knock on Barry's office door anyway.

"Come in!" he yelled.

I flinched, and then opened the door.

"Hi. I'm in your class. I'm Rick Lax."

"Take a seat, Mr. Lax."

As I did, I realized that I hadn't prepared enough material for a sit-down conversation and that I probably shouldn't have taken Barry up on his offer.

"What can I do for you?" he asked.

Fortunately, during my stint as a *Michigan Daily*[58] writer, I had learned how to generate an endless supply of questions on the spot to keep interviewees from feeling as though I hadn't adequately prepared.

"Just dropping by to say hi and introduce myself—Professor Dewey said it was a good idea. Have a lot of students been dropping by?"

"You're the first," Barry said.

Barry had his bat leaning against his desk. Maybe, I wondered, to discourage students from dropping in to say hello.

"Tell me about yourself, Mr. Lax."

"Like where I'm from?"

"Where are you from? What college did you go to? Do you have a girlfriend?"

"Michigan, University of Michigan, and no girlfriend."

"My godson goes to Michigan. Good undergraduate program, *great* law school."

*Thanks.*

"But you're wrong about one thing," Barry said. "For the next year, the American legal system will be your girlfriend. She will demand your time and your undivided attention."

"Actually, I have a date this Sunday."

[58] The University of Michigan student newspaper.

"With your casebook?"

I paused.

"With a girl."

"That makes you a cheater, Rick," he said with a half grin, "and you will pay for it."

Barry smiled.

"I'm being a little facetious here."

"I was wondering—"

"Good meeting you, Mr. Lax," he said, standing. "See you in class."

I closed the door on the way out and then found Devenpeck's office. His door was partially open, but I knocked anyway.

"Yes?"

I poked my head in.

"I'm Rick Lax. I'm in your Legal Writing class."

"I remember you; there are only eight students. Can I help you with something?"

"Just wanted to drop by and say hi."

"Oh," he replied. Then, "Come in."

As a sign of respect, I decided to turn my cell phone off, and then, since it seemed like the right thing to do, I set it on Devenpeck's desk so he could see that it was off.

He stared at my phone as if it were staining the wood.

"Should I take if off?" I asked.

"Let me ask you a question, Mr. Lax: would you set your cell phone on your boss's desk?"

"I guess that would depend on what kind of relationship I had with my boss."

As soon as I said it, I regretted it.

"And what kind of relationship," Devenpeck continued, "do you think *we* have?" He paused. "Kindly remove your phone from my desk."

I removed it.

As soon as the opportunity presented itself, I excused myself and rolled my stuff out of Devenpeck's office, out of the law school, up Michigan Avenue, and to the Second City Health Club, where I could sweat out the embarrassment.

After forty minutes on the elliptical machine, I found my locker and dialed my combination. My lock didn't open.

A small thread of panic.

I tried again: nothing.

In frustration, I yanked my lock as hard as I could.

It popped open.

Slowly, I opened the locker. I didn't see my laptop, but I did see why the club paid a security guard to hang out in the locker room. After all, theft is a biggie in Chicago. Happens all the time—especially here in the downtown area.

"Did you see somebody go into my locker?" I asked the ancient security guard.

"What?"

"I said, did you see somebody go into my locker?"

"You're going to have to speak up."

*"Did somebody go in my locker!?"*

"Jesus! You don't have to shout; I'm standing right here. Now what's the problem?"

"The problem is that somebody broke into my locker

and stole my computer. You didn't see somebody breaking the lock?"

The locker was right in his line of sight.

"I didn't see anything," the guard said. I showed him my lock and he said, "It's broken."

*Thanks.*

"It wasn't broken an hour ago."

"Let's go fill out a police report," the guard said, as if this sort of thing happened every day, which, for all I knew, it did.

I was pissed. I punched the locker. I wanted to sue somebody, only I didn't know whom. I couldn't sue the health club because they had "WE ARE NOT RESPONSIBLE FOR LOST OR STOLEN GOODS" signs posted on every flat surface. I couldn't sue the thief because (1) I didn't know who he was and (2) theft isn't a civil offense. I couldn't sue the lock manufacturer because, well, okay, maybe I could have sued the lock manufacturer, but I didn't think of that at the time. I'd only been in school for a week. At the time, all I could think to do was punch the locker a second time.

# CHAPTER THREE

## Playing by the Rules

On Saturday, Marty gave me his first-week notes. On Sunday, I bought a "Great Quality" laptop for $500. I won't bore you by listing all the reasons why the name Great Quality was ironic, but I will tell you that the computer's fan sounded like a lawn mower. My parents weren't happy about buying me a second laptop after just one week of school, but they appreciated that the theft wasn't my fault. I appreciated that most people couldn't get back on their feet as quickly as I did after sustaining such a devastating theft. I let my parents know how grateful I was and they told me to just keep focused on school.

Sunday night, I took April to a cheesy romantic comedy, where, as planned, we sat in the front row and talked through the whole thing, except for those two seconds when we kissed. It was a bad kiss—so much so that we spent the majority of the post-movie portion of our date joking about how bad it was.

The second one was better.

On Monday, I wore my complimentary XL DePaul T-shirt to Con Law . . . as did Dan and two of the other serious students. I figured we'd all run out of clean clothes at the same time.

"Looking good, Rick," said Dan.

"You, too." I turned to Nadeeka, who wasn't wearing a shirt, and said, "It's DePaul T-shirt day. You didn't get the memo?"

She hadn't.

"Congratulations," Dan said.

"On what?"

"Your scholarship. You got the shirt with the scholarship, right?"

*The shirt went with the scholarship. Ah.*

"You mean they didn't make you pick between the two?"

At the start of the semester, everybody must have assumed a handful of Section 2 students just happened to buy the same ill-fitting DePaul law school T-shirt. By the second week of class, most people had figured out what the T-shirts meant. By that week, wearing the shirt was no longer considered just a fashion misstep; it was considered a statement about the wearer's refusal to hide or apologize for her intellectualism.[59]

At that moment, I realized that Nadeeka had already

[59] My first experience with T-shirt politics came in the seventh grade: Kids gave shirts away at their bar mitzvah parties (as it is written in Deuteronomy 5:19), and on subsequent Mondays all the kids who had attended the parties wore the shirts to class, making it clear which losers weren't invited. According to my mother, this infuriated the PTA. The PTA moms, mine included, agreed that they wouldn't let their children give T-shirts away at their parties. So, for a few months, kids gave away do-rags and scrubs instead. Many Mondays in early 1995, the popular West Hills seventh graders looked like motorcycle-riding Jewish surgeons. By the time my own bar mitzvah rolled around, several of the PTA moms had already violated the pact, so my mom said that I could violate it, too.

figured out what the T-shirt meant, which was why my memo joke had been received so coldly; she thought I was mocking her for failing to score a scholarship herself.

I didn't care for Nadeeka, but I did feel the need to apologize.

"Sorry about the T-shirt joke. I just realized what the T-shirts mean."

*"Right."*

"Seriously."

"Don't worry about it; everybody's being a bitch to me today. One of Erik's Angels called me a 'heifer.'"

"No, she didn't."

"Not to my face; she was talking to another one of the Angels. I overheard her. Anyways, you people can all kiss my fat ass."

Professor Laurel taught us about the Commerce Clause of the Constitution, which gives the United States government power "to regulate Commerce with foreign Nations, and among the several States, and with the Indian Tribes." Laurel continued to teach us about the Commerce Clause for the next two months.[60]

On Tuesday, Professor Barry taught us more about *mens rea.*

"Today, we're going see how *mens rea* pertains to statutory rape."

---

[60] So if I don't mention Con Law much in the next fifty pages, it's because it wouldn't interest you, unless you own a multi-state milk pasteurization corporation, in which case I apologize for the omission.

Barry glared at us as if we had all committed the crime.

"In Illinois, statutory rape is a strict liability offense. You know what that means? It means that it has no *mens rea*. It means that even if an underage girl said she was over the age of consent and the defendant believed her, he's still guilty."

Erik raised his hand and asked, "What if the girl lies to you and tells you she's above the age of consent?"

"Guilty!" said Barry.

"Creep," Kimberly muttered. I didn't say it at the time, but I thought Erik's question was totally legitimate.

"Many of you might already be aware of this," Barry said at the end of class, "but elections are coming up next week. We need to pick a Student Bar Association representative for the section. The SBA rep reports to the Head Dean, makes announcements to the class, and sends e-mails to the entire section. If you're interested in running, stop by the SBA office before Friday and let them know. A week from today, all the candidates will give short speeches—we're talking three minutes or less, people. I'm going to be timing them. And then you'll all vote by secret ballot. Any questions? No? Good."

Barry had kept us eleven minutes over, which left four before Ryder's class. I rushed to the SBA office and declared my intention to run. The upperclassman SBA rep took my name down and wished me luck. I'd need it: eight Section 2 students had already signed up to run,[61] Kimberly Mitsuya included. Section 1, by comparison, had only two candidates so far.

That night, April called and asked if I wanted to see an improv show at the Del Close Theater. I told her that I did but that I couldn't because I had to learn about the Uniform Commercial Code's *implied warranty of merchantability.*[62]

"You're turning me on again," she said.

"Some other night," I said.

Forty-five minutes into my reading, I realized that I was retaining none of it. I couldn't stop thinking about April, and eventually I called her back and said, "Let's go."

"The show started ten minutes ago."

"Then let's do something else. Come over to my apartment and we'll figure something out."

We didn't. When April showed up, in an ironic and disappointing reversal I couldn't stop thinking about the UCC. She kept suggesting activities and I kept saying no. Eventually she asked, "Well, what do you want to do?"

"I really don't know."

---

[61] It wasn't the first time I'd found myself in the middle of a multi-party election. Back at the University of Michigan, I ran for Ann Arbor City Council as an Independent in a three-way race. I got 24 percent of the vote, losing to the Democratic incumbent, who had been living in the city decades longer than I had. In retrospect, I didn't stand a chance—no non-Democrat does; as of December of 2006, the ten-member Ann Arbor City Council is 100 percent Democrat. There used to be a Republican on the council, but he changed parties to keep his seat.

[62] *Implied warranty of merchantability:* the implicit guarantee that a merchant's goods are "reasonably fit" for the purposes for which they are sold.

"Well, you're no fun tonight."

By the time April left my place, I was too tired to complete my reading.

Barry's prophecy had proven true.

All the SBA candidates wore suits on the day of the election, except for me. I wasn't trying to pose as the populist candidate; I just didn't think to wear one.[63] Kimberly Mitsuya had plastered the Lewis Center's student lounge with professional-looking campaign posters featuring herself standing before an American flag and gazing off into the distance. Erik, who was also running, passed out "Vote Erik" stickers and got three of the cool kids to wear "Vote Erik" sandwich boards. One candidate baked chocolate-chip cookies for the entire section, but so did another candidate, thus splitting the coveted cookie-lover vote.

Kimberly volunteered to speak first. As the only minority student in the running, she held a distinct advantage over the rest of the field simply by standing out. She carried a bucket up to the front of the classroom, paused theatrically, and then emptied out a pile of colorful erasers in the shapes of lips and ears.

Kimberly's campaign manager handed out the erasers while Kimberly spoke.

"When I was young, my mother told me, 'Kimberly, you have one mouth and two ears, so I suggest you listen twice as

[63] So maybe I was the populist candidate after all.

much as you speak.' If you elect me as your section representative, I promise to do just that."

*Ridiculous. She's got no chance.*

"I promise to listen to your concerns, and I promise to speak on them. Who will I speak with? Whoever will listen. You can't imagine it right now, but down the road, there will be a call for leadership. And when that call is sounded, I'll be there for you."

*No chance at all.*

One of the cookie bakers, the second of the two female candidates, spoke next. She said that she recorded every lecture and that if we voted for her, she'd make the recordings available to us.

I dismissed her as a one-issue candidate.

Erik gave the most professional stump speech in that it was the vaguest. He spoke about "doing what is right" and being "a voice for the *entire* section," and he emphasized the word "entire," as if certain segments of our eighty-person section had already experienced inadequate representation. The kids wearing the "Vote Erik" sandwich boards snickered throughout his speech, infusing his words with the subtext *vote for me because I'm not a humorless career politician like Kimberly Mitsuya.*

*This will be a tough act to follow.*

I spoke second to last: "For those of you who don't know me, my name is Rick Lax, and I also want to be our section's SBA representative. I spoke with a few SBA upperclassmen, and they told me that even though an SBA rep can't make any big changes to the way things work, small changes are possible. So that's what I want to talk about over the next two minutes: small changes. . . ."

Presenting myself as the "issues candidate." I talked about professors holding us overtime and about the busted hinges on Room 815's chairs—on mine, at least.

"Thanks for listening, and if you do vote for me," I concluded, "then thanks for that, too."

Professor Barry tallied the votes.

The eraser stunt worked; Kimberly won.

After the election, a handful of students walked up to me and said that they thought I spoke well, that they voted for me, and that they couldn't believe Kimberly had won with such a cheesy, patronizing speech.

"Now, now," I chided, "this is not the time for internal strife. We must admit defeat and unify behind our elected section representative, who, need I remind you, is Kimberly. Let us put our differences behind us and work together in the spirit of cooperation."


I've been called a lot of things in my life,[64] but never a racist—until the week after the SBA rep election, when it happened twice. *Esquire* editor at large A. J. Jacobs says that journalists should find three particular incidents of a certain occurrence before labeling the occurrence a "trend" and writing a story about it.[65] I'm just at two—I haven't been called a

---

[64] For example, "immature," "insensitive," "egotistical," "obnoxious," etc.

[65] Which, according to Jacobs, is why his "Trend of Two" column never caught fire.

racist since the following two incidents occurred—so I can still beat the journalists to the punch and tell you that RICK LAX IS A RACIST, but I'm not going to do that because I'm not. And even if I were—*which I'm not*—it wouldn't be evidenced by the two incidents that occurred the week after the election.

The first incident occurred outside of Barnes & Noble. I was on my cell phone with my dad, complaining about Devenpeck, when a man approached me.

"If I were to talk to you right now, would it be a racial issue?"

The man was black and he was asking a decent sociological question, but he had interrupted my conversation mid-sentence to ask it.

"It's not a racial issue; it's a rudeness issue. I'm talking to my father right now."

My dad asked what was going on, and as I tried to tell him, the interruption continued, "I guess it is a racial issue—huh?"

"Sir, can I help you with something?" I asked.

I figured hearing the guy out might be the only way to get rid of him.

The man pulled five or six CDs from his backpack and asked if I wanted to buy one.

"No thanks," I said, and returned to complaining about Devenpeck—at least I tried to.

"Why does everything always have to be a racial issue with you white students?"

"Our conversation is only a racial issue in that you're trying to sell me your CDs by playing the race card."

The man paused, then pointed his finger at me.

"You're a damn racist!" He looked to a group of nearby students from Section 3. "We got a racist here!"

Maybe he was hoping I'd say something like: "I'm not a racist. And to prove it to you, I'm going to buy every single CD you've got. In fact, I'm so not a racist, I insist on paying double! Now tell those students how much I love black people." But I didn't, and the man walked away, muttering, "Damn racist," again and again.

The second incident occurred two days later. Dan had invited Marty and me to join the serious students for lunch. I knew Nadeeka would probably be there, but I still agreed to come, figuring I'd come away with a good story at the least.

Yep, she was there. Now, Nadeeka is Sri Lankan, which, apparently, gives her the right and obligation to speak on behalf of all nonwhite people, but especially black people. Or perhaps she thought dating a black guy gave her this right. Probably the latter, given how much she talked about reparations and how little she actually talked about her boyfriend, aside from mentioning him in passing (e.g., "Well, I'm dating a black guy, so . . ."). Basically, Nadeeka used the word "plight" in every fifth sentence.

We went to a nearby pub, and over the course of lunch, which was even more topical and politically charged than I had expected, I actually found myself agreeing with much of what Nadeeka was saying, but I would have willingly sacrificed my most deep-seated beliefs to avoid saying, "I agree with Nadeeka on that last point."

Our meeting of minds couldn't last.

"I didn't expect there to be so much racism in our class," Nadeeka announced. This came out of left field for me, as I had never picked up on any racism in our class.

"What racism did you detect?" I asked as innocently as possible.

Nadeeka correctly identified my question as a challenge.

"When Professor Dewey walked through the door on the first day of class, everybody gasped. Everybody was in a total state of shock."

Professor Dewey is black and sports a buzz cut, so her appearance did distinguish her from our other professors, but we were in downtown Chicago, where we passed lots of black female professionals—many of whom sported buzz cuts—every time we walked to class.

"For the record," I replied, "I didn't hear anybody gasp, let alone everybody."

Dan chimed in and tried to change the topic. I suspect he foresaw there was no way in hell Nadeeka could defend her allegation, and unlike me, he didn't want to watch her struggle to do so. Nadeeka didn't let Dan change the topic, but she also didn't defend her initial claim.

"I heard one of our classmates—I'm not going to say who—say, 'Professor Dewey must not spend much time blow-drying her hair.' Tell me that's not a racist comment."

"You *could* say the same thing about a bald white guy," I pointed out.

"Well, maybe *you're* a racist."

Okay, so Nadeeka didn't call me a racist so much as she said that I might be a racist, but given the tone of her suggestion, she may as well have come out with the direct accusation. Then again, not doing so was probably a clever way of avoiding defamation charges.

"I'm not going to dignify that with a response," I replied, which I immediately recognized as an inherent contradiction. Fortunately, Nadeeka didn't pick up on that.

"Figures."

"I don't see any racism inherent in the comment."

I gave Nadeeka the benefit of the doubt by accepting that the event had actually occurred and that Nadeeka had reported it accurately.

"That's because," Nadeeka said, "you're probably a racist yourself."

"I'm sorry," Marty said, "but I need to jump in here. Rick's not a racist, and you're way out of line in calling him one."

"I see how it is; you're *both* racists."

For a liberal, Nadeeka sure reminded me of Joseph McCarthy. She turned to Dan and asked, "Am I wrong?"

"What you're saying is . . . serious stuff," Dan replied.

"You're not answering my question; I asked if I was wrong."

"Nadeeka." Dan removed his Buddy Holly glasses and leaned in. "I understand you're passionate about this topic. We all know that. And I'm not saying I think you're wrong or right; I'm just saying that before you call somebody else a racist, you really have to think through—"

"Will nobody back me up here?"

Nadeeka looked around the table. Everybody except me avoided her gaze.

"You know what? Forget it," Nadeeka said. "None of you know what you're talking about."

Nadeeka slapped a ten and a five on the table and then stormed out.

Yes, the blow-dryer comment probably had been motivated by race. The anonymous classmate might have said the same thing about a white male, but he probably wouldn't have. But that doesn't necessarily make him a racist—does it? Do all comments motivated by race or having racial overtones make the speaker a racist? Of course not. What makes a person a racist, as I explained previously, is being called a racist three times.

Dan never invited Marty and me to have lunch with the serious students again.


"I have some great news for you!" Devenpeck said. "You're getting your first legal research assignment today."

We all looked at one another. Was he serious?

"That means you all get to spend some quality time in your favorite place: the law library!"

Nope.

"Can everybody say, 'Thank you, Professor Devenpeck'?"

One student could and did. Devenpeck wasn't amused.

"Cheer up," Devenpeck continued. "It'll get worse. This

week's research assignment should only take you an hour or two."

Most law schools' writing programs teach students to do legal research on westlaw.com or lexisnexis.com because, well, that's how it's done in the real world. My father says that almost everybody at his firm does legal research online, including the seventy-year-old partners. The one person at my father's firm who does legal research the old-fashioned way is my father, who insists that the firm pay thousands of dollars every year for hard copies of massive, obscure taxation publications like the *Commerce Clearinghouse Standard Federal Tax Reporter* and the Bureau of National Affairs' *Tax Management Portfolio* series, even though their online counterparts are much cheaper and take up no space. Only because my father is a senior partner do the younger associates tolerate his Luddite demands.

The DePaul University College of Law's legal writing program does not teach computerized legal research. Devenpeck told us we weren't even allowed to do online research for the entire first semester and that doing so would constitute an honor code violation.

"To complete your assignment," Devenpeck said, "you'll all need to use the same few library books, so I'd like to direct your attention to section 12.4 of the Student Handbook." Devenpeck opened his dog-eared copy. " 'It shall be a violation of this Code to do any of the following: Damage, hide, or otherwise exert unauthorized control over any library property or class-related materials.' When you're done with a book, put it back on the shelf right where you found it. Don't put me in the position of having to guess whether you hid it on purpose or simply forgot to put it back."

"Has that actually happened before?" Cassandra asked.

"No, I was just saying that for my health," Devenpeck said.

Devenpeck divided the class into groups of twos, and I got paired with Adrienne.

"If you have any questions or concerns, ask your partner—that's what they're there for. That said, you don't *have* to work with your assigned partner; I just strongly recommend that you do. But just because you're allowed to work with a partner doesn't mean you're allowed to divide research tasks. Dividing tasks is an honor code violation. Both of you have to be involved in every research step."

"Lastly," Devenpeck said, "I'd like to bring section twelve point seven to your attention: 'Failure to Report Violations.' 'It shall be a violation of this Code for a student to fail to report any suspected violation of this Code where such student has reasonable grounds to believe that such a violation has occurred.'"

Adrienne and I agreed to meet in the law library at four on Friday. She suggested we exchange phone numbers in case anything came up, and I reminded her that we had already exchanged numbers the night of orientation.

"Was I drunk?"

Adrienne looked concerned, as if maybe something more had happened between us.

"I called you to tell you that I had your credit card . . . at McFadden's. . . . I gave it to Erik for you."

"Oh, that was you. Sorry, what's your name again?"

*Ouch.*


They don't call Chicago the Windy City for nothing. They call it the Windy City because after the Great Chicago Fire of 1871 the city planners remodeled the Loop using a grid system, creating high-velocity wind tunnels throughout the downtown area, but especially the area between my apartment building and the law school.

Six weeks into my first semester, the wind picked up, the temperature dropped, and my classmates' collective spirit dropped with it. The cold wreaked havoc on Marty's health. Before he walked into Crim Law one Thursday, I didn't know somebody's entire face could be chapped.

"I feel like I look," he said.

Marty felt certain his sister, who was visiting, had given him a cold, and that his mother, who was also visiting, had given him a fever. To me, that seemed unlikely—wouldn't the cold and fever cancel each other out?—but given how bad he looked, anything was possible.

"I didn't do my reading," Marty said. "I'm falling behind in every class."

"Did you tell Professor Barry?" I asked.

On the second day of class, Barry had said that if we were ever unprepared, we should set a note on his podium before class began, saying (1) our first and last name, (2) that we were unprepared, and (3) the reason why we were unprepared.

"I'll take my chances," Marty said.

Barry had assigned eight short rape cases that spanned a hundred years and illustrated how the *common law*[66] crime of rape had evolved into modern-day sexual assault. Under the common law, courts would only find a defendant guilty when his victim could prove that she had kicked and screamed and put up a big fight and that the defendant had overpowered her. Today courts look for freely given consent; it's accepted that victims don't always fight back because some fear that resistance might provoke further violence, while others experience "frozen fright," a nervous system shutdown that makes resistance impossible.

Under the common law, a man could not legally rape his wife. Courts have since done away with this marital exception. Also under the common law, many states had "corroborating evidence" requirements, which meant that the State needed to produce evidence (like semen or bruises) beyond a victim's testimony to convict a defendant of rape. This requirement has also been done away with.

I found the *Boro v. Superior Court* case most interesting of all. The defendant, Daniel Boro, called the victim and introduced himself as Dr. Stevens. He told her that he worked at Peninsula Hospital, that he had just gotten her blood test

[66] *Common law:* the unwritten law, based on custom and usage within the courts.

results, and that she had contracted a "dangerous, highly infectious, and perhaps fatal disease." There were two ways to treat this disease, "Dr. Stevens" told her. For $9,000, she could undergo a painful surgical procedure followed by six weeks of uninsured hospitalization. Or she could have sex with an "anonymous donor" who had been injected with a disease-curing serum and would transfer it to her, presumably through his semen.

Naturally, the latter approach required no hospitalization and would only set the victim back $4,500. She went for option two, and Daniel Boro was eventually found out and charged with rape accomplished by "fear of immediate and unlawful bodily injury." The California court ruled that while some deception such as *spousal impersonation,*[67] can be grounds for rape, Boro's scheme, while despicable, was not rape.

When we got to the *Boro* case in class, Professor Barry called on Marty, pursuant to Murphy's Law.[68]

"Mr. Rockhind, can you tell us the facts of the *Boro* case?"

Marty couldn't; he just sat there like a deer in the headlights.

"Mr. Rockhind, the facts? Can you tell us about *Boro?*"

---

[67] *Spousal impersonation:* pretending to be somebody's spouse and sleeping with them.

[68] Fact: the first known reference to Murphy's Law is found in the September 1928 issue of *The Sphinx,* the premier magician's magazine of the day: "It is an established fact that in nine cases out of ten whatever can go wrong in a magical performance will do so. The great professors of the art are not immune from the malignancy of matter and the eternal cussedness of inanimate objects."

"I'm sorry, I didn't do my reading. I've been really sick."

Barry cleared his ears with his pinkies, as if he couldn't hear what Marty was saying.

"Was I unclear when I said that you are to come to every class prepared to discuss the assigned reading? Was I unclear, Mr. Rockhind, when I said that if you are unprepared, you should put a note on my podium explaining why?"

Barry waited patiently for Marty to give an audible answer.

"No," Marty said.

"Does anybody here think I was unclear when I said those things?"

Silence.

"Mr. Rockhind, as for your sickness: if you are healthy enough to come to class, you are healthy enough to have done your reading."

Marty nodded.

"I'm going to call on you at the beginning of our next class, and either you will be prepared to answer my questions or I will lower your grade one half point. Does that sound fair?"

Marty nodded again.

Nadeeka raised her hand.

"Was something unclear, Ms. . . . Ms. . . ." Barry examined his seating chart.

"Sangarapillai," Nadeeka offered.

"Yes, Ms. . . . Yes, was something unclear?"

"No. I just wanted to tell you the facts in the *Boro* case."

"Save it for next week," Barry said, turning his gaze on Marty. "We're out of time."[69]

The only thing worse than spending Friday afternoon at the law library doing research is spending Friday afternoon at the law library waiting for your partner to show up so you can begin doing research. Adrienne finally appeared at the library's fifth-floor entrance forty minutes after our four o'clock agreed meeting time. She didn't apologize—not unless you count "I don't have that much time, I have friends coming into town in like an hour, so we have to get this thing done ASAP" as an apology. I don't, personally. I count it as whatever the opposite of an apology is.

"Okay, but I don't want to rush through anything," I said, even though Adrienne had just, essentially, said she meant to do exactly that.

"Let's just get started. Did you get my message? About me running late?"

"No."

"Whatever, let's just get started."

---

[69] FIRST-YEAR TIP: When you're unprepared for class, the absolute worst thing you can say when called upon is, "I'm unprepared." If you think law professors appreciate that kind of forthrightness, you're wrong. When they call on you, they want to see you perform; they're trying to prepare you for the courtroom environment, where you'll be expected to perform for a judge. Acting as if you've done your reading when you haven't may be unethical—outright lying about it surely is—but professors will often forgive misstatements you make in class as long as you make them with gusto.

Adrienne and I scanned the instructions, then retrieved the appropriate *American Jurisprudence* legal encyclopedias, *West Digest System* books,[70] and *Shepard's* updating books.[71] We culled specific bits of information from each and recorded what we found in our workbooks. By 6:30 P.M., we were halfway done. Devenpeck's one-to-two-hour time estimate had been way off.

"This is a problem," Adrienne said.

"Yeah, there's no way we're going to finish this in the next hour."

"Then it's time for plan B: you get the *Federal Reporters*[72] for questions ten through twelve; I'll get the *Illinois Reporters* for thirteen through fifteen."

"Devenpeck said we couldn't divide research tasks."

Adrienne looked at her watch.

"What are you talking about? I don't remember anything about dividing research tasks. I'm going to the fourth floor to find the *Reporter* for question thirteen. You can do whatever you want."

I wanted to get out of the library as much as Adrienne did—probably more; I'd been there forty minutes longer than she had. But I wasn't about to violate the honor code; I wanted us to continue on to question 10 together. Because

---

[70] The books that organize legal issues and cases by topic for easy identification and cross-identification.

[71] The books that say whether cases have been overturned or whether they're still "good law."

[72] The books that contain case opinions.

that wasn't an option, I followed Adrienne down to the fourth floor to find the *Illinois Reporter* for question 13.

We completed the assignment by 7:45 P.M. Specifically, we competed *an* assignment by 7:45 P.M.; as Adrienne photocopied her workbook pages, I noticed that we had done exercise M, which I had assumed would be followed by exercise M-2 but was actually followed by exercise M-1, the exercise we had been assigned.

"Are you fucking joking me?" Adrienne said, as if I were solely responsible for the error. "Okay, here's what we're going to do: we're going to turn this in and pretend like we didn't notice. Devenpeck will have to give us the points."

"What gives you the impression that Devenpeck would give us a single point for turning in the wrong assignment?" I asked. "He'd give us nothing."

"Really?"

"Of course he would. Plus, what if he asks us whether we knew we did the wrong assignment?"

"He's not going to ask us that."

"But what if he does? Then we'd either have to lie, an honor code violation, or have to admit that we knew we did the wrong assignment."

"None of that is going to happen."

"But what if it does? This is how students get expelled."

"I can't be doing this. I can't be doing this," Adrienne said to herself. "This is fucking ridiculous."

Adrienne called her visiting friends and told them she'd meet them at her apartment in half an hour.

"I'm not turning the wrong assignment in," I told her.

"Fine. We'll come back and do the right assignment in a few days. Let's do it on Tuesday. We'll meet here around seven. Seven is good."

*It is? For whom?*

"Tomorrow works better for me."

"Well, I can't do it tomorrow."

"Then how about Monday afternoon around—"

"Let's just do it on Tuesday."

"Adrienne, I can't do it on Tuesday. I have—"

"Let's do this on our own then."

"Fine by me."

Adrienne and I finally found something we could agree on.

Later that night, April and I took the Red Line to the Del Close Theater, just across the street from Wrigley Field, to see some improv comedy. About a minute before the show started, April turned to me and said, "We need to talk."

I knew whatever we needed to talk about wasn't going to be good. Nobody ever says, "We need to talk. You've got fantastic skin. What do you use?"

"What do we need to talk about?" I asked, trying to keep the panic out of my voice.

"I've . . . been lying to you about something."

As a magician—*but not as a law student or as a future attorney*—I lie to people all the time. I've been doing it since I was four. It comes naturally to me. I regularly look people directly in the eye and say, "There's no way I could know what card you picked," even though I'm 100 percent positive they picked the three of clubs.[73] Because I lie so often, *as a magician,* I've come to think of myself as a human lie detector. In practice, that doesn't mean I'm better than the average person at detecting lies, only that when I find out that somebody has been lying to me, I'm extra-surprised.

"What have you been lying about?" I asked.

"My age. I'm not twenty-one."

*Okay. . . .*

"And I'm not twenty."

*Please stop there.*

"And I'm not nineteen."

*Oh, God, please . . .*

"I just turned eighteen. I just graduated from high school."

Then the lights dimmed and the improv began.

The emcee entered, welcomed everyone to the show, and then pointed directly at me.

"What's something interesting you said today? Some bit of dialogue from your life."

April's revelation had left me in shock.

"Or maybe something you wanted to say, but didn't for whatever reason. . . ."

The words just came out: "Why did you lie to me?"

As the comedians improvised on "Why did you lie to me?" April quietly cried. The show ended and April told me, "If you never want to see me again, I'll understand."

I told her that I was hurt, but that her age didn't bother me as much as her deception did. April said that she had

[73] Every card in the deck is the three of clubs.

only lied because she was afraid that if I had known her real age, I wouldn't have even asked her out.

She was probably right.

We walked from the theater to Uncommon Grounds, a late-night coffee house, and I asked her if she had lied about anything else.

"No, and you don't have to be such a jerk about this," she said.

"Given the circumstances, asking if you lied about anything else is fair game."

She thought and then said, "You're right."

At 11:30 P.M. she got a call and turned red.

"I have to go," she said.

"Is everything okay?"

"I have to go *right now*."

"What's going on?"

"Never mind. I just have to go."

Walking to the car, she got a second call.

"I'm out shopping with some friends," she told the caller, and hung up.

"I've got the right to know what's going on."

"I'm way past curfew," she said. "My dad's flipping out. If I don't come home this second, I'm grounded. He'll do it, too; he's such a jerk sometimes!"

Yes, eighteen is just a number, but April wasn't just eighteen years old; she was also an eighteen-year-old—one who like totally didn't want to get punished.

Now's probably a good time to mention that I never slept with April. And that before we had even met she had reached Illinois's age of consent. But if April had been a little younger, if our relationship had gone on a while longer, and if she had never come forward with the truth, I might have wound up on the wrong side of the witness stand with a state prosecutor like Professor Barry telling a jury of my peers that strict liability offenses like statutory rape have no *mens rea*.

The day after the improv show, April and I got together at the Barnes & Noble café where we first met and agreed that it'd be best for us to not see each other again. Erik was in the café, too, studying Civ Pro. After April walked out, I told Erik, who had apparently gotten a good look at April, what had just happened. He told me I'd made the wrong choice because, as he put it, April was "magically sexlicious."

I replied, "She's eighteen, you pervert," and immediately realized that I was being only half-facetious and that ending things with her was probably the right thing to do.

Cassandra was in the café, too. Erik asked me to go over to her table and convince her to come to his friend's house party on Saturday. I said I'd try.

"What would I do there?" Cassandra asked. "I don't drink."

"There's more to do at house parties than just drink," I said.

"Like what?"

"Lots of things."

"Such as . . ."

"Watching other people get drunk."

"On Sunday I have to wake up at seven for church. Why don't you take that girl you were just talking to?"

"Because she's eighteen."

That was the first time I ever heard Cassandra laugh. I liked the way it sounded.

I took the Brown Line to Southport, walked a few blocks south, and then up a rickety wooden staircase to Erik's friend's apartment. The party looked like a typical undergrad house party: there was a group of people smoking a hookah in the corner, a group of people sitting on a couch watching *Harold and Kumar Go to White Castle,* a group of people sitting around a table and playing a drinking game called Waterfall, and a group of girls—the ones Nadeeka had dubbed "Erik's Angels"—standing around in the kitchen. The Angels were gossiping about Cassandra:

"She thinks she's better than us."

"She always talks about people behind their backs."

And about Nadeeka:

"What a bitch."

"She's so angry."

"And you know she acts that way because she's *so* fugly."

Erik handed me four Natty Lights and I joined the Waterfall game.[74] Judging by the pile of empty beer cans on the ground, the group had played a few rounds already. After twenty minutes, the game ended and the group moved to Erik's friend's balcony to smoke. I didn't go, so I'm not

[74] See Appendix B.

sure whether the group smoked tobacco or marijuana, but when they came back in, they asked me to show them some magic tricks. The Waterfall cards were sticky, so I messed up a few sleights, but nobody caught anything.[75] The group wanted to see more and more, so I dipped into my B-material and then my C-material. Nobody caught anything.

"That's fucked up."

"That's some fucked-up shit."

"You're like the next David Copperfield."

"Here's what you need to do," Erik said. "You need to drop out of school right now and become a magician."

"Try telling that to my dad."

"You *need* to."

What I needed to do was sleep. So I left.

There's no way Cassandra spent the entire night reading Contracts. I found that out Sunday morning when I read the assigned *Vokes v. Arthur Murray, Inc.* case—it was just three pages long.

Audrey Vokes, a widow of fifty-one years, attended a party at Davenport's School of Dancing, during which the owner of an Arthur Murray franchise called her an "excellent dancer" and sold her eight half-hour dance lessons. During the lessons, Vokes "was influenced by a constant and continuous barrage of flattery, false praise, excessive compliments, and panegyric encomiums, to such extent that it would be

[75] Which makes me think it was probably marijuana.

not only inequitable, but unconscionable, for a Court exercising inherent chancery power to allow such contract to stand." Vokes had purchased 2,302 hours of dance lessons for a total amount of $31,090.45.[76]

Vokes was told that she possessed "grace and poise," that she was "rapidly improving and developing," and that additional lessons would "make her a beautiful dancer, capable of dancing with the most accomplished dancers." A sucker for flattery, she kept buying more and more. In reality, the Arthur Murray instructor thought that Vokes had no "dance aptitude" and that she had "difficulty hearing the musical beat."

Generally, to rescind a contract on the grounds of misrepresentation, the misrepresentation must be one of fact, not opinion. But here the court found that "it should have been reasonably apparent to defendants that [Vokes's] vast outlay of cash for many hundreds of additional hours of instruction was not justified by her slow and awkward progress, which she would have been made well aware of if they had spoken the 'whole truth.'" The court found the misrepresentation of opinion was great enough to rescind the contract.

Sometimes Professor Dewey called on people and other times she asked for volunteers. That Monday, she asked for a volunteer and, as had happened many times before, Nadeeka was the only person who raised her hand. Often she would be called on, but this time Dewey ignored her. The professor

---

[76] This case took place in 1968. $31,090.45 in 1968 equals roughly $200,000 in 2008.

patiently scanned the classroom for another volunteer. Nadeeka raised her hand higher and moved it from side to side.

"I see you, Ms. Sangarapillai, but let's give somebody else a chance to participate in class today."

"Oh, snap," said Erik, a little too loud.

"Are you volunteering yourself?" Dewey asked Erik.

"Just clearing my throat. Sorry about that."

Cassandra raised her hand and put her alleged Saturday night studying to work. It was the first time she had spoken in class. She did okay, but Dewey never interrupted her or asked her any follow-up questions.[77]

On Tuesday, Barry began class just like he said he would: "Mr. Rockhind, please tell us about the facts in *Commonwealth v. Sherry*."

Marty, looking much less chapped, frantically flipped through his Crim Law book.

*"Commonwealth v. Sherry?"*

*This won't be pretty.*

Barry's eyes widened; this time he really couldn't believe what he was hearing.

"Mr. Rockhind, I assume you're prepared for today's class."

"I am. I mean, I thought I was. I just don't remember the *Sherry* case."

---

[77] FIRST-YEAR TIP: Some professors call on students, some ask for volunteers, and some do both. If your professor does both, always volunteer at least once, and do it toward the beginning of the semester. That way, if you ever get called on when you're unprepared, your professor won't see you as an unprepared student; she'll see you as a sometimes-unprepared student.

"Perhaps page three fifty-one will refresh your memory."

Marty turned to page 351, looked confused, and said, "This case was from last week's reading."

"Yes, Mr. Rockhind. *Commonwealth v. Sherry* was one of the two cases we didn't get to last week, and I'd like to get to it now."

"I thought you wanted me to do *this* week's reading."

"Mr. Rockhind, have you *still* not done last week's reading?"

Marty turned white. But Barry didn't go for his bat; he just sighed. That wasn't necessarily a good thing for Marty. When your parents raise their voices at you, you know you've done something wrong, but when they're quiet, they mean business.[78] Barry meant business, too: he took a silver pen from his breast pocket—it had been resting there, untouched, all semester—and made a small mark on the seating chart next to Marty's name, presumably a skull and crossbones.

"Would anybody else like to take the case?" Barry asked.

Nadeeka shot her hand up again.

"You want to give it a go?"

"Sure!" Nadeeka responded, with the enthusiasm of an *Annie* understudy who had just been informed that the lead had come down with a sudden, suspicious case of food poisoning.

After class, I wanted to console Marty, only I didn't know how. I couldn't exactly say, "It's no big deal," because

---

[78] My high school band teacher Mr. Ambrose used this analogy to show how quiet music can be more powerful than loud music.

it was. I couldn't say, "You'll get another chance," because he probably wouldn't. So I asked if I could buy him a beer.

"No thanks. I'm heading to the library. Got to get back on the horse."

I left the school to find a new, more secure gym. What I found was the Chicago Fitness Club. The club's motto is "Experience the difference. — Experience Chicago Fitness." I couldn't tell if the referred-to difference was the seven-story rock-climbing wall, the in-house sushi bar, or the $145.00 deep-tissue massage, but not having to exercise in a sub-sub-basement was difference enough for me. Yes, the Chicago Fitness Club cost more than twice as much as the Second City Health Club did, but when I factored the cost of my stolen laptop into my Second City membership, the Chicago Fitness Club was a bargain.

I sat down with a personal trainer who asked me embarrassing personal questions like "Were you looking to tone or bulk up?" and "Which parts of your body would you most like to work on?"

"I'm just looking for a place to work some stress off. I'm a law student. . . ."

That came out wrong; it sounded like I was bragging.

The trainer poured on the flattery: "Really? A law student? Well, for a law student, you're in fantastic shape."

"Thanks."

"No, seriously. Most of my friends in grad school eat nothing but pizza and burgers. You must eat really healthy—it shows."

If the guy wasn't trying to sell me a gym membership, I'd have assumed he was hitting on me.

"How often do you work out?" he asked.

"I try to do at least five sessions a week."

"Well, keep it up, man. Keep it up. You're looking good."

The trainer's flattery won me over, and like Mrs. Vokes, I was ready to buy whatever he was selling, which, in this case, was a $120-per-month gym membership. He pulled a one-page contract from his filing cabinet.

"Here's your contract, Mr. Lawyer."

Now that I'd had a little training in the fine art of contracts, I took a few minutes to read through this one, clause by clause. Number 7 piqued my interest:

> If the Member, because of death or disability, is unable to use or receive all services contracted for, the Member, or his estate as the case may be, shall be liable for only that option of the charges allocable to the time prior to death or the onset of disability. *CFC shall in such event have the right to require and verify reasonable evidence of such death or disability.*

"Mrs. Lax, I understand that the tragic and untimely loss of your only child must have been devastating. But unless you produce a corpse, I'm afraid you'll have to pay his membership fees through the end of December."

If somebody fakes their own death to get out of their membership, shouldn't the club just let them go? Was this a big problem for the Chicago Fitness Club? Was it happening often enough that their lawyers felt it necessary to add clause 7 to their standard contract? Was this how contract law was actually done?

The trainer had no authority to negotiate particulars and I wanted to work out, so I signed on the dotted line, did thirty-five minutes on the StairMaster, and took my stuff— all my stuff—back to my apartment.

On Wednesday, I went back to the library to do my Legal Writing assignment. I got stuck on question 4, which required a certain volume of *Words and Phrases* that wasn't shelved where it should have been. I went through the spines one by one, but the one I needed simply wasn't there. I searched the library for Legal Writing classmates of mine who might be using the book. Half an hour later, I gave up and skipped to question 9.

An hour before class, I returned to Professor Devenpeck's office and knocked on his half-open door. He opened it a few more inches.

"Can I help you?"

"I can't find the *Words and Phrases* I need."

"Mr. Lax, if I were your employer, would you barge into my office like this[79] and ask me that?"

"If I were doing my first research assignment? Yes. I think so."

Wrong answer.

"Not very professional, Mr. Lax. What does your research partner think you should do?"

---

[79] Again, I did knock.

That was a tricky question; if I told Devenpeck that Adrienne and I had gone our separate ways, he might ask why, and then I'd be forced to either tell him about Adrienne's wanting to divide research tasks and turn in the wrong assignment or lie. I didn't like the idea of being known as "the Section 2 snitch" for the next three years. Plus, the honor code said that failing to report an honor code violation is a violation in itself, so I myself might be in violation.[80]

Luckily, Devenpeck didn't wait for my answer: "Are you saying you think somebody hid the book?"

"I have no idea what happened to the book. I just know that it's not where it should be."

"Mr. Lax, if you can't complete questions four through eight, I can't give you points for them."

"So, what should I do?"

"I suggest you find a different law library and see if they have a copy of the volume you're looking for."

Devenpeck started to close his door.

"But class starts in an hour," I said.

He opened it back up.

"And whose fault is that? You should have dealt with this earlier, Mr. Lax."

Devenpeck returned to his lair.

I turned the assignment in, incomplete, hoping that

---

[80] I'm pretty sure I wasn't, though, because Adrienne hadn't actually violated the honor code; I stopped her before she could—on two separate occasions. The honor code didn't say anything about reporting honor code violation attempts.

Devenpeck and his TA, a squawky girl named Kiki, could at least read my borderline illegible handwriting for the questions I was able to answer. During class, as Devenpeck taught us how to use apostrophes to show possession—apparently you put an apostrophe and then an *s* after the word—Kiki skimmed through our assignments to make sure that everybody had turned one in and had completed every question.

At the end of class, Kiki jumped up and announced, "I need to see Student 985352 after class." Those were the last six digits of my DePaul student identification number. To preserve anonymity, we didn't put our names on our legal writing assignments; we used our student ID numbers. I assumed Kiki wanted to squawk to me about questions 4 through 8, but I was wrong:

"We need to talk about your ID number," Kiki said.

She threw my research assignment across the table and it landed on my lap.

"What's wrong with my ID number?" I asked.

"Why don't you hold your assignment up and look on the back?"

Our confrontation felt like an interrogation scene from an old cop movie.

"Do you notice anything about its placement?" Kiki asked.

"No."

"Nothing at all?"

"If you could just tell me what I did wrong, I'll fix it for next time."

"You don't notice anything wrong with the placement of your ID number?"

"Is it supposed to go on the upper left?"

I had put it on the upper right, just below the staple.

"No. . . ."

"Is it supposed to go above the staple?" I asked.

"*Yes,*" Kiki said, and she said it as if it were the most obvious thing in the world.

"Okay. I'll put it above the staple next time."

"Do you know why it's supposed to go above the staple?"

"No."

"Because when I check to make sure that everybody turned their assignment in, I put the stack of papers face-down on the table and spread them out like this"—Kiki demonstrated—"and if your number is below the staple, I can't see it because the assignment on top of it covers it up."

Playing by rules like Kiki's is, to a large degree, what practicing law successfully is all about. Every jurisdiction and every court has its own unique procedural and formatting requirements, and ignoring them can result in the dismissal of a case. For example, Federal Rule of Appellate Procedure 27(d) reads as follows:

(1) *Format*
*Paper Size, Line Spacing, and Margins.* The document must be on 8½ by 11 inch paper. The text must be double-spaced, but quotations more than two lines long may be indented and single-spaced. Headings and footnotes may

be single-spaced. Margins must be at least one inch on all four sides. Page numbers may be placed in the margins, but no text may appear there.

If lawyers succeed by following specific procedural guidelines, musicians succeed by breaking them. After Legal Writing, I got a call from Rob from Tally Hall, who told me that his bandmate's song "Good Day" had just won the BMI Music Foundation's John Lennon Scholarship for songwriters.

"Good Day" is structured like a traditional pop song,[81] but it breaks the traditional pop mold in two significant ways: (1) the meter bounces from 8/8 to 5/8 and back to 8/8 during the verses and then settles in at 4/4 for the prechoruses and choruses,[82] and (2) the key moves from A during the verses to F# during the prechoruses, and the main chorus is in C.[83]

But Rob hadn't called to brag on his bandmate's behalf; he wanted to know whether the band could spend the following two nights at my apartment. They had a gig at a Wicker Park club called Double Door and needed a place to stay.

"You can definitely stay here. I just wish you would have given me a little more notice."

---

[81] Verse, prechorus, verse, prechorus, chorus, verse, chorus, bridge, outro.

[82] By comparison, most traditional pop songs stay in 4/4 meter the whole time.

[83] By comparison, many traditional pop songs stay in the same key the whole time and follow simple I–IV–V chord patterns (e.g., "Great Balls of Fire," "The Lion Sleeps Tonight," "Louie Louie," "King of Spain").

"Sorry about that, but sometimes we don't even figure out sleeping arrangements until after our gigs. Last week after this show in the Bronx, we drove around until four A.M. looking for a motel, and the only one we could find was called Holiday Hotel—not Holiday Inn—and when I asked about rooms, the guy at the front desk gave me an hourly rate. And each room had only one bed. We ended up getting two rooms, and they both had red and gold wallpaper, and heart-shaped mirrors, and bottle openers attached to the walls."

"See, I think it's awesome that—"

"Oh, and we were solicited by prostitutes on our walk from the parking lot to the hotel. Sorry, you were saying . . ."

"It's awesome that you guys live so spontaneously."

It occurred to me at that moment that if I had stuck with magic, I might be living the same spontaneous, carefree—

"I think it's awesome that you get to sleep in a room without semen on the ceiling."

*Touché.*

# CHAPTER FOUR

## Two Sides to Every Story

The bookstore was packed on Saturday, so I headed to Argo Tea on Pearson and Rush to study Crim Law. I found a seat between two girls, one of them a petite redhead, the other wearing a tight black-and-white-striped sweater, looking as though she'd just escaped from the Calvin Klein clink. (This is the sort of thing I think up when I'm supposed to be studying Crim Law.)

I finished up the *mens rea* and rape unit, and then the fugitive, with whom I had been making small talk, tapped my arm.

"Can you watch my stuff," she asked in a thick Czech accent, "while I use the bathroom?"

She wanted me. I knew that because (1) asking girls to watch my stuff while I use the bathroom was how I hit on them and (2) the fugitive took her cell phone and purse into the bathroom with her, leaving on the table just her diary and pen, which nobody was going to take.

While she powdered her nose, I prepared a monologue about how a seven-foot-tall, four-hundred-pound thug had tried to steal her stuff, until I kicked his ass. At that moment, a boy walked into Argo asking for money. Nobody gave him anything, and he asked the petite redhead if he could sit down across from her and rest for a moment. She said okay. After a minute or two, the boy thanked her, stood up, and walked out the door. Ten seconds passed before the redhead began frantically looking around her table, on the floor, and in her backpack. She bolted out the door, yelling, "Somebody stop that kid!"

Theft is a biggie in Chicago. Happens all the time—especially here in the downtown area. Through the window, I saw the redhead, who was wearing chunky brown shoes, trying to chase after the boy. Without too much thought, I leaped out of my seat and chased the kid down Rush, past Pippin's Tavern, Downtown Dogs,[84] and a Checks Cashed. I followed him west onto Chicago and flew past a discount perfume store, AmeriCash Loans, Beck's Book Store, Soupbox, Jimmy John's, Fantasy Nails, and Starbucks. I finally caught up to him and grabbed his jacket in front of the McDonald's next to the Chicago Red Line L stop. The kid handed the redhead's phone over without a fight.

And then he took off again, but he didn't get very far.

I grabbed his jacket again and this time I didn't let it go.

"Kid, if *I* can catch up to you in two and a half blocks, you shouldn't be doing this."

"I'm sorry."

He was barely audible. He looked pitiful.

"You think saying you're sorry is going to make this okay?"

---

[84] Downtown Dogs' walls and cashier counter are covered with photos of canines. I doubt Downtown Dogs is consciously trying to suggest their hot dogs are made from actual dogs, but that's how it comes off.

"I was going to sell it and buy food with the money."

As I debated whether I believed the kid, he broke free once again, and when I caught up to him, once again, he started to fake cry. I'd shed a few fake tears myself back in the day,[85] so I know a fake cry when I see one. I wish I could have said the same about the crowd of onlookers, which was growing bigger and bigger. As the street magician had taught me, nothing attracts a crowd like a crowd. The onlookers hadn't seen the kid steal the phone; all they saw was a twenty-three-year-old brute grabbing a defenseless, crying child by the jacket and threatening him. When I felt a hand come down on my shoulder—it came down *hard*—I can't say I was surprised.

"Let the kid go."

I turned around and saw a man of Professor Barry's height and build standing behind me.

"This *kid* stole some girl's cell phone." I pointed the word "kid," as if his theft disqualified him from minor status.

"Let the kid go," the man repeated.

"Did you hear what I said? He stole a girl's—"

"Did *you* hear what *I* said? Let. Him. Go."

I let him go.

"I'm going to take over," the man said.

"What do you mean, you're going to 'take over'?"

"I'm going to take over. Just go away, and let me handle this."

That's when I realized the man and the kid might have

[85] The day = college.

been working together. Now, I'll chase a kid down a crowded street while it's still light out, but I won't fight a man twice my size. Bringing the redhead's cell phone back to Argo would have to be victory enough. Besides, I stood no chance of convincing the crowd that I was the good guy and the kid was the bad guy. And as the street magician taught me, when your show's bombing, end it.

I returned to Argo, where I delivered the cell phone and the redhead managed a "my hero."

*All in a day's work for Lawyer Boy.*[86]

That would have been the perfect opportunity to ask the girl for her phone number—she'd pretty much have to give it, even if she was married or a nun—but the number I wanted was the Czech fugitive's. Out of earshot of the redhead, I said to the fugitive, "This would be the perfect opportunity for me to ask that girl for her phone number—right?"

"Definitely."

---

[86] Several months after this happened, David Copperfield bested three more would-be thieves. In Palm Beach, three teenagers approached the magician's car after a gig. Copperfield assumed the kids wanted autographs, but what they wanted was his personal belongings. The magician's assistants emptied their purses and gave the kids their passports, plane tickets, cell phones, and over $500 in cash. Copperfield turned his pockets inside out and showed them to be empty, so the kids left. But his pockets weren't empty; they contained his cell phone, wallet, and passport. Copperfield had defeated the thieves with magic.

"Call it reverse pickpocketing," Copperfield told the *Palm Beach Post.*

Because one of the magician's assistants had written down the thieves' license-plate numbers, the kids were later caught and brought to justice.

"The thing is, I don't want her number; I want yours."

She gave it to me. And if you think that line was cheesy, you should have seen the napkin tulip I made for her.[87]

In November, the Windy City got windier and the Michigan Avenue crowds thinned. We wrapped up jurisdiction in Civ Pro and the Commerce Clause in Con Law. With final exams looming, my classmates formed study groups. Each group had at least one connection to a second- or third-year student who could provide it with old class notes and exams.[88]

Another benefit of joining a study group was psychological. After ten weeks of school, we still had no real way of knowing how well we were doing. Outside of Legal Writing, we didn't write papers, turn in assignments, take exams, or get any feedback. We had no way to compare ourselves to our classmates, and because we were going to be graded on a curve, their progress relative to our own was the only thing that mattered.

The *DePaul Law Review*, the school's student-run law journal, would only take students from the top 10 percent of the class. The biggest law firms in Chicago wouldn't so much as

[87] See Appendix C.

[88] FIRST-YEAR TIP: Studying in groups is fun and social, but studying isn't supposed to be fun or social. That studying in groups is so palatable should tell you something. You know how you prefer the elliptical machine to the treadmill? That's because it's easier and doesn't burn as many calories. You know how much you love eating muffins for breakfast? That's because muffins are cake and not a legitimate breakfast food. Studying in groups is fun because it's not studying. Every hour you spend studying in a group is an hour you could have spent actually studying. Find another way to get your hands on upperclassmen's old notes.

glance at the résumés of students who weren't in the top 15 percent of their class. Decent midsized law firms wouldn't consider students who weren't in the top 30 percent of their class,[89] even though—and I think this bears repeating—half of the Section 2 students were going to get below-average grades.

Most of my classmates weren't used to getting below-average grades. They weren't used to having to compete against so many equally motivated students. They didn't know how to deal with the competition, so when study groups came along and gave them a seemingly productive forum to share how unprepared they all felt, they jumped at the opportunity.

I didn't jump because I believed that the feeling of security study groups provided was false and potentially detrimental.[90] So I just had to feel insecure and live with it. Yes, DePaul was paying for most of my education, but I still had a lot invested in my law school performance (e.g., my life, my future, my identity), and I had no idea how well I was

[89] These numbers vary with the school; a Harvard student at the seventieth percentile of her class would have little trouble walking into a six-figure job after graduation.

[90] Let's say I joined a study group of four and after a week it became apparent that I was the most prepared one in the group. I might then falsely conclude, whether consciously or subconsciously, that I was more prepared than most of the students in Section 2. And then, based on that conclusion, I might cut back on my studying. But maybe the group I had joined contained the three biggest slackers in Section 2. Maybe I was the most prepared student within the group, but the fourth-least-prepared student in Section 2. Mathematically, my sample size (my study group) in this hypothetical situation was too small to allow me to make an adequate judgment about my placement in the class.

performing. Before law school, I hadn't taken my studies too seriously. Come to think of it, before law school, I hadn't ever felt so nervous about anything. I'd worried about losing *control*[91] of spectators' cards or splitting double-lifts in two, but those sleight mistakes could be covered up through misdirection and outright lying. Outright lying couldn't change a law school C to an A; it could only change a C to an honor code violation, which the Dean of Internal Affairs could then change into an expulsion. Presto-chango!

Then there was the caffeine. In undergrad, I drank coffee while doing my homework, but my undergrad readings weren't that long and my textbooks weren't that big. By comparison, in just over two months the weight of my law school textbooks had ground the wheels of my rolling bag down to nubs. Some days my reading regimen topped a hundred pages. I spent an average of four and a half hours a day reading, which translated into three Starbucks grandes.

According to the Stress, Anxiety, Depression Confidential Helpline:

> Caffeine can exacerbate or even cause stress, anxiety, depression, and insomnia because it interferes with a tranquilizing neurotransmitter chemical in the brain called adenosine. This is the chemical that turns down our anxiety levels—it's our body's version of a tranquilizer.
>
> Caffeine docks into a receptor for adenosine and regular

---

[91] *Card control:* techniques for keeping track of spectators' cards while shuffling and cutting the deck.

use of caffeine is enough to produce anxiety and depression in susceptible individuals.[92]

The coffee did nothing to improve the sleep I wasn't really getting in the first place. I studied most nights until eleven or midnight, watched an hour or two of television, fell asleep around two, and then woke up at 7:45 A.M. the next day. In other words, I was sleeping less than my dad.

With just over five hours of sleep per night, my concentration plummeted. Sometimes I read long Con Law passages and retained absolutely nothing—not even the topic. My readings took longer and longer, so I got to bed later and later, and so on and so on.

My dad reassured me that my fears and anxieties were normal. He said that he remembered having the same feelings before his first-semester finals.

92

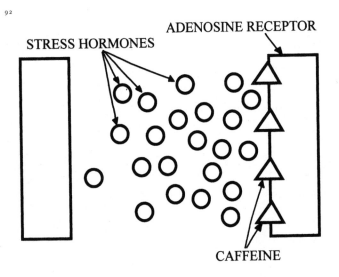

STRESS HORMONES

ADENOSINE RECEPTOR

CAFFEINE

"I was particularly scared of my roommates," he told me. "One of them did his undergrad at Princeton and the other one did his undergrad at Yale."[93]

My father did his undergrad at Wayne, a state college located in the heart of downtown Detroit.

"Long story short: we all ended up in the middle third of our class. I don't remember who got what, but I remember we were all pretty close. Of course, I had to study twice as hard as those guys to get there. Speaking of which, don't you have some studying to do?"

"This is your first actual writing assignment," Devenpeck told us. "From this point forward, your assignments will get longer and more complex." He paused. "This is the point where you all groan and say, 'Really?' "

Nobody took the bait.

Devenpeck handed out a packet of legal documents from a fictitious case called "In the Interest of Maran Montgomery." He directed out attention to the "Motion for a Declaratory Judgment," seeking a declaration that Maran Montgomery is a Navajo Indian protected by the Indian Child Welfare Act, which contained the following Statement of Facts:

[93] After graduating from law school, the guy who had done his undergrad at Yale went to work at a prestigious New York law firm. My father headed to a small firm on 12 Mile (four miles from Eminem's 8), thinking he'd never see his Ivy League classmate again. He was wrong; my father ran into his former roommate at a drugstore on 11. The classmate had returned to Michigan after just one year in New York, to work at a small firm on 10.

Growing up, Polly Laurich lived with her mother on a Navajo reservation in southern New Mexico, where she regularly participated in traditional Navajo activities such as rug weaving and basket weaving. Polly ran away from her mother and to Chicago in 1994, when she was seventeen.

Polly Laurich gave birth to a girl, Maran Montgomery, on April 15, 2005. Maran Montgomery is one fourth Navajo. On March 21, 2005, the Department of Children and Family Services took custody of Maran, and then Circuit Court Judge Jean-Pierre Delacroix determined that Maran Montgomery was an abused/neglected child. The Court placed Montgomery in an Aurora foster home. On November 24, 2005, Judge Delacroix heard from the Navajo tribe and determined that 1) Maran Montgomery in an Indian child within the meaning of the Indian Child Welfare Act and 2) the ICWA applies to the proceedings.

Before you get too attached to Polly Laurich and the Navajo tribe, you should know that our assignment was to argue, on behalf of the State, that Maran Montgomery was not an Indian child under ICWA and that she should stay with her non-Navajo foster parents in Aurora. Specifically, we had to create a Statement of Facts that would portray the situation in a light less favorable to the Navajo tribe and more favorable to the State.

When Devenpeck handed our previous assignments back at the end of the last class, I saw that he had made good on his promise to give me no points for questions 4 through 8.

Still, my grade was above average—actually, all of my Legal Writing grades had been above average. I didn't understand much of what Devenpeck said in class, but apparently my classmates' lack of understanding trumped mine, and like I said, that was the only thing that mattered.

As I was walking home from class, one of my rolling bag wheels popped off. It was only a matter of time. I returned to the luggage store with the broken bag and an arsenal of basic contract law terms. I felt confident that I could argue my way into a refund or a replacement bag at the least. I failed to consider that my jury, the person who would determine whether I got my money back, was also the defendant, the person from whom I wanted the money. I barged into the store and demanded to speak to whoever was in charge. The lady standing behind the counter wearing an orange *khimar* nodded.

"I bought this bag two months ago and it just fell apart."

I pointed to the corner of the bag that had held the wheel.

The woman counter-pointed to a tiny sign taped by the door: "ALL SALES ARE FINAL."

"Nobody showed me that sign when I bought this bag, and nobody told me that all sales were final, and, even if they had, the bag still falls under the UCC's implied warrantee of merchantability." Whatever that meant.

The woman pointed to the sign again, said something in what sounded like Arabic, and threw her hands up.

"Look, the Uniform Commercial Code governs the sale of this bag. Are you with me so far?"

She wasn't; more Arabic.

"Well, I'm never buying anything from this place again,"

I said, and walked out. Maybe I should have threatened to take her to small claims court. Then again, learning when to turn away losing cases is just as important as picking winners.

I stopped in every department store on Michigan Avenue but couldn't find a comparably priced bag. Michigan Avenue retail shops don't cater to students; they cater to tourists who come to Chicago for the sole purpose of getting ripped off. Every rolling bag I found cost at least $150. That's why, the next day, I went back to see my new friend.

"I need another bag," I told her.

She laughed and showed me to the rolling bags.

"You want the same one?" she asked.

Her English was just fine.

"The cheapest one you've got."

The cheapest bag was also the largest—ludicrously so. I took it.

That evening I had plans with the Czech fugitive, whose name turned out to be Victoria. We met back at Argo, where we planned to do some work before meeting her roommate Chelsea at the Signature Lounge, a touristy bar on the ninety-sixth floor of the Hancock Building.

"How about this," Victoria suggested. "We spend the first forty minutes flirting and then the next fifty working, and then we'll head to the bar."

"Okay," I replied, "but if the first part goes well, we play footsie while we work."

"Who decides whether the first part goes well?"

"I do," I said, hoping she wouldn't ask why.

"Why? I'm the girl. I get to decide."

"Fine," I said, working out the appropriate language in my head. "We can condition the footsie on your subjective personal satisfaction as long as you use a good faith standard in making your determination."

"What?"

"You haven't read *Gibson v. Cranage*?"

"Must have missed that one."

"This guy agreed to paint a portrait of this other guy's dead daughter with the understanding that he could refuse to accept the painting if it wasn't satisfactory to him."

"And was it?"

"No, but the guy with the dead daughter refused to say why, so the artist sued him. The court said that the guy with the dead daughter didn't have to say why he didn't like the painting. In other words, contractual liability can be conditioned on subjective personal satisfaction."

"That's really interesting."[94]

After forty minutes, Victoria said the flirting went well, so we played footsie as I browsed through the notes prepared by Maran Montgomery's caseworker Joanna Campion, who conducted interviews with Maran's mother, Polly Laurich. I took the most incriminating facts from the interviews and worked them into a fact pattern that would best serve the State's goal of keeping Maran Montgomery's case out of the Indian Child Welfare Act:

[94] Victoria, I later learned, was minoring in theater.

Polly Laurich started drinking at the age of thirteen, and started smoking marijuana at fifteen. At seventeen, she ran away from her home and began working as a "personal masseuse," though Laurich refused to explain what that entailed. Laurich has been arrested for possession at least three times, and arrested for prostitution at least twice.

During Laurich's last court-ordered in-patient drug treatment program, she met Buster Montgomery, who she went on to marry. Laurich says that Buster "drinks even more than [she does]" and that he occasionally hits her with a flyswatter.

Polly and Buster had a child, who, because Polly's mother is allegedly a Navajo Indian,[95] is one-quarter Navajo. Maran Montgomery, the child, was born prematurely. She weighed six and a half pounds and tested positive for cocaine. After the test results came in, the court found probable cause that Maran was an abused/neglected child.

The court placed Maran in a foster home, where she is now doing well—all things considered. Polly seeks to take Maran back using the Indian Child Welfare Act, even though Maran has never been on a Navajo Indian

[95] Note how I buried this unavoidable, Navajo-favorable detail in the middle of a sentence.

reservation, is unaware of her alleged Navajo heritage, and is not living with a Navajo family.

I showed Devenpeck's Statements of Facts and my own to Victoria.

"Which one do you think is right?" she asked.

"They're both right. Two sides to every story."

"I'm not talking about correct; I'm talking about *right*."

My professors hadn't devoted much time to discussing who was "right" or "wrong," partially because in almost every case both parties are right about some things and wrong about others. The lawyer's philosophy is, let the philosophers argue right and wrong; we've got work to do. Lawyers don't ask, "Who is right?"; they ask, "What are my client's objectives, and how can I best accomplish them?"[96]

"Let me put it like this," Victoria said. "Who would you take as a client?"

"Whoever walked through my door first."

"But who would you rather take?"

"Whoever could pay me more."

"You're joking—right?"

"Am I?"

Was I?

Afterward, we walked across Michigan Avenue to the

[96] If you have a problem with that, take it up with the Model Rules of Professional Conduct. Lawyers aren't supposed to judge their clients— that's what judges and juries are for.

Signature Lounge. Victoria maintained a distance of five or six feet. Every time I'd try to get closer to her, she'd move farther away.

"Am I contagious?" I asked.

"You're not supposed to use a rolling bag unless you're over forty or going to the airport. Even then you wouldn't need one that big."

"There's no law student exception?"

"Can we just pretend you're going to the airport?"

"Okay."

Victoria took my hand in hers, and whenever somebody passed by she'd say, "We'd better hurry up or you're going to miss your flight!"

The first thing Victoria's roommate said when she saw me was, "What's with the bag?"

"It's for my flight," I managed. "To New York."

"Rick's a fixer-upper," Victoria said.

Victoria's roommate asked how we'd met.

"I asked Rick to watch my stuff while I used the bathroom. When I got out, he was gone. Five minutes later, he came back all sweaty, and acted as if he'd saved the day by leaving my stuff unattended. Then he asked for my number."

Two sides to every story.

The next Crim Law unit was on drugs and possession. Drug cases, most of which are nonviolent, don't have the inherent drama of murder and rape cases, but they're still important. About two million Americans are behind bars, and a quarter of them are there for nonviolent drug offenses.

Half the people I knew in undergrad smoked marijuana,[97] and half of those marijuana smokers used other illegal drugs, too. Many of the guys in my Crim Law book—always guys— were sentenced to decades in jail for doing the same thing my college peers did, the main difference being that the guys I read about in my Crim Law book had been caught, usually more than once.

Professor Barry taught us that you don't have to literally possess drugs to commit the crime of possession. "Look at 5/4-2: 'Possession is a voluntary act if the offender knowingly procured or received the thing possessed, or was aware of his control thereof for a sufficient time to have been able to terminate his possession.' In other words, if you're at a party where people are smoking pot, and you stay at the party, you're guilty of possession."

In Contract Law, Dewey taught us *Krell v. Henry,* a

[97] I didn't run with a dangerous crowd; I ran with poli-sci and theater students (each group being less dangerous than the other). The usage rate among my college friends reflected the liberal political atmosphere of Ann Arbor. While attending the University of Michigan, I lived catty-corner to a head shop called Shiva Moon, which was four or five doors west of a store called 42 Degrees, which claimed to have the largest glass pipe selection in the country. 42 Degrees was just four doors down from Stairway to Heaven, a second-story head shop. And Stairway to Heaven was right across the street from the Diag, the place where Hash Bash, the largest annual marijuana legalization rally in the Midwest, is held.

British case that dealt with *frustration of purpose.*[98] C. S. Henry wanted to rent a flat from Paul Krell in Pall Mall, London, to see the coronation of Edward VII. Henry and Krell's contract didn't contain any express reference to the coronation, but Krell understood that Henry wanted the place to see the king. When Edward VII fell ill and the coronation date changed, Henry refused to pay for the flat and Krell sued to enforce the contract. The *Krell* judge said:

> In my judgment,[99] the use of the rooms was let and taken for the purpose of seeing the Royal procession . . . and I think that the words imposing on the defendant the obligation to accept and pay for the use of the rooms for the manned days, although general and un-conditional, were not used with reference to the possi-bility of the particular contingency which afterwards occurred.

In other words, the judge let C. S. Henry off the hook.

After class, I had to grab a quick lunch, print out my Legal Writing assignment, and turn it in before class began. Devenpeck graded late assignments down one whole point and, as he liked to say, "If it's not at my podium before class begins, it's late."

I would usually print out my Legal Writing assignments

[98] *Frustration of purpose:* a defense to a charge of nonperformance used when an unexpected event causes a defendant to not do whatever it is she said she'd do.

[99] Duh.

the night before they were due with my apartment building's business center printer. Only that printer was busted, and even though I'd spent an entire summer working in the Maddin, Hauser copy room, I couldn't fix it. I had to use DePaul's printers, which I hadn't yet attempted, so I didn't yet know that printing documents at the computer lab was a Byzantine ten-step process involving the creation of user names and passwords[100] and, since nobody was around to walk me through the steps, I had to figure them out by trial and error, which took thirty minutes.

I didn't have time for lunch, but I was able to print the documents and get to class with minutes to spare. Like two of them.

Devenpeck gave us our next assignment. We were to write a full memorandum of law arguing that Maran Montgomery was not an Indian child and that the ICWA did not apply. We were supposed to fix up our fact patterns and use them as the first section of the memo.

Cassandra raised her hand.

"So we're not going to get our fact patterns back until we turn the full memo in?"

"Bingo," Devenpeck replied.

"Then how will we know what to fix?"

"You'll find out in two weeks."

"But that's when our assignments are due!"

"Very good, Ms. Winston. Now were there any other questions?"

---

[100] Note the plurals.

Cassandra had two: "How are we supposed to do this?! How are we supposed to do any of this?!"

"Allow me to clarify: were there any other legitimate questions?"

There weren't.


I planned to start my memo Friday night, but Victoria called me at six and invited me over to play poker—"first with chips, and then, if things go well, per my subjective satisfaction, strip"—at her place, a third-floor Pottery Barn–esque apartment in Lakeview.

Victoria did what nobody else in Chicago could do: she took my mind off law school. Unfortunately, she didn't do it consistently; even while doing shots of Effen Black Cherry Vodka and playing strip poker with her, I couldn't stop thinking about my ICWA memo and about finals. At least, that's my excuse for losing so badly.[101]

So I sat there losing. I thought, *If law school is going to bring my poker game down, it should bring Victoria's down, too.* I started to tell her about frustration of purpose and about the crime of possession: "If you're in a room with drugs in it, and you know about them, and you have a chance to leave, but you don't, you're guilty of possession."

"You're guilty of possession," Victoria repeated.

"Exactly."

---

[101] Of course I could have cheated. Of course I could have dealt seconds and bottoms, stacked the deck, or switched in a cooler. But ever since I got caught cheating in a euchre game by my Hebrew school youth director when I was eleven years old, I vowed to never cheat at cards again.

"I wasn't clarifying; I was putting you on notice."

"Huh?"

"I'm telling you, you're guilty of possession right now. You have a chance to leave my room, don't you? And you're still here."

"What do you have in your room?"

"Want to see?"

"No."

I managed a tentative laugh.

Victoria walked over to her dresser and removed a Muppet Babies lunch box. She set it on the bed, about a foot from me, and opened it up.

"It's not going to bite you."

"Please put it back."

"Okay. I'll put it back. . . ."

Victoria closed the lunch box up, but she didn't put it back; she chased after me with it.

"Put it back!"

"It's coming for you!"

"Get it away!"

"It's going to get you!"

I ran out of Victoria's room and slammed the door behind me.

She came out thirty seconds later, sans lunch box.

"Do you do a lot of drugs?" I asked.

"Not since I quit dealing."

When Victoria was ten, she and her parents emigrated from the Czech Republic to a suburb north of Chicago. Her parents both found work as bank tellers. When Victoria got into Northwestern, her parents were proud that their only child had gotten into such a prestigious school but heartbroken that they couldn't afford to send her there. So she promised her parents that she'd find part-time work right after classes got started. The part-time work that she found was drug dealing. Her then-boyfriend/drug dealer got her started.

"What did you deal?"

"Not heroin."

"But what *did* you—"

"Everything except for heroin."

"I suppose that's one way to pay for college."

"Paid for half."

"How'd you pay for the other half?"

"I'll tell you when you're older."

I paused.

"Okay, I'm older."

"Seriously, I will tell you. Just not now."

"Just tell me you weren't a hooker."

She slugged my shoulder.

"That's a no?"

"I wasn't a hooker!"

"Okay, okay, you can tell me later then."

"Are the drugs going to be a problem for you?" Victoria asked.

"I don't think the Committee on Character and Fitness would like it if I got caught with your stash."

"Are you being serious? If you are, you're the most paranoid person I've ever met. It's not like the cops are going to barge into my apartment for no reason."

"Can we just hang out at my place from now on?"

"Fine."

I fell asleep around three and woke up at four—to a knock at the door.

"Victoria."

I shook her by the shoulder.

"Somebody's at the door."

The knocking grew louder.

"It's just Chelsea," Victoria said to me, and then "What do you want?!" to Chelsea.

Louder still.

"Come in!" Victoria yelled.

"I locked the door before we went to sleep," I said.

"Why'd you do that?"

From behind the door: "Open up!"

It wasn't Chelsea; it was a man.

"It's Chelsea's boyfriend. Please just go open the door."

"This is the police! Open up!"

"Oh my God, oh my God, oh my God, oh my God, oh my—"

"Rick. Chill. It's Chelsea's boyfriend. He's just messing with us."

I flipped on the nearby lamp and saw the lunch box on Victoria's dresser. The lid was open, and it looked like one of the bags was open, too.

"Last chance! Open up this door in ten seconds or I'm going to open it up for you!"

"Actually," Victoria said, "that doesn't sound like Chelsea's boyfriend."

"Oh my God, oh my God, oh—"

"Ten! Nine!"

I hopped out of bed and dashed over to the dresser.

"Eight! Seven!"

I collided with the dresser and knocked the lunch box onto the ground. A mushroom cloud of white powder drifted to the ceiling.

"Six! Five!"

"It's snowing!" Victoria declared. She got out of bed, put out her arms, and twirled around, shouting, "Wheee! It's cocaine Christmas!"

"Four! Three!"

I used my hand as a broom to sweep the powder under the dresser, but our faces were already caked white like a couple of Noh dancers.

"Two! One!"

*Thwack. Thwack.*

Four police officers broke the door down and barged into Victoria's room, guns drawn.

"Get your hands where I can see them!"

I raised my hands above my head. A trail of white powder followed.

The officers pulled Victoria off the bed and threw her onto the floor next to me. They twisted our arms around and handcuffed us to each other. It didn't take them long to find the lunch box.

"Do you know what the penalty for possession in the state of Illinois is?" one of the officers asked.

"I forgot," I said.

Professor Barry appeared at Victoria's door, baseball bat in hand.

"You forgot?!"

"I didn't know we were supposed to memorize—"

And then I woke up.

It was just before one. Victoria was still asleep, so I climbed on top of her.

"Good morning," she said.

"Afternoon," I corrected.

"Mmmmm . . . more sleep."

"It's almost one," I said. "I'm supposed to have done two hours of studying by now."

"Mmmmm," she cunningly countered.

"You can go back to sleep," I said, "but I have to get out of here and get to work. Got to study Crim Law."

"But breakfast!"

"I'll just have a protein bar. I've got one in my bag."

"But what about me?"

"I'm sure you'll find something to eat."

"I want us to eat together."

"I can't. I'm sorry."

"But I want to eat together."

I looked at the clock. Victoria looked at me looking at the clock. It was ten to one.

"Fine. Go," she said.

I could tell she was pissed about my abrupt departure, but I really did have to go; I had to read sixty-five pages.

To a non–law student, sixty-five pages probably doesn't sound so bad, but it is. Law school pages aren't like the ones you had to read for your undergraduate sociology class—the ones you could skim while watching *Real World* and doing shots of cheap tequila off your roommate's sister's navel. Law school pages are tough. *Federalist Papers* tough. The margins are tiny and the font is small. They're filled with abstract concepts and peppered with Latin legal phrases like "prima facie."[102] They're designed to stop speed-readers dead in their tracks.

I learned to speed-read in 1997, after seeing *Good Will Hunting*. At the time, I didn't understand that Hunting read so fast to fill his huge brain; I thought speed-reading made his brain huge, and that it could do the same for mine, which, in turn, would somehow win me a girl like Minnie Driver. I never took a course or seminar on speed-reading, but I did read three books on the subject. I increased my reading speed by a factor of three without decreasing my comprehension.

The problem was, coming into law school I'd been speed-reading for almost a decade. I'd completely forgotten how to read at a normal speed. It made me easy to spot at the beach (I was the one reading John Grisham using my fingertips to underline each line of text with machine-gun rapidity), but because my law school pages were too dense for speed-

---

[102] *Prima facie:* Latin for "on its first appearance." Prima facie evidence, unless rebutted, sufficiently proves a proposition.

reading, I was forced to go through them at my non-speed-reading reading speed, which, because I was so out of practice, had dropped far below my pre-speed-reading reading speed.

So at my sub-pre-speed-reading reading speed, I trudged through sixty-five pages of Crim Law, which covered accomplice liability. Basically, if, either before or during a crime you do anything to help a criminal, you become her accomplice. You can also become an accomplice by doing nothing; in *People v. Crutcher*, the court ruled that a defendant who had watched a crime "without disapproving or opposing" was "more likely than not" an accomplice. *People v. Ruiz* confirmed this much:

> If the proof shows that a person was present at the commission of the crime without disapproving or opposing it, it is competent for the trier of fact to consider the conduct in connection with other circumstances and thereby reach a conclusion that such person assented to the commission of the crime, lent to it his countenance and approval, and was therefore aiding and abetting the crime.

You can even be convicted for dating the wrong person; in *People v. Shaw*, the defendant and codefendant were "hitting on each other," and the court felt the flirting made them "companions," and therefore accomplices. The only way to get out of accomplice liability is to withdraw from the crime. According to *People v. Ellis,* a withdrawal is only effective if the defendant terminates her conduct before the offense is committed and she neutralizes the effect of her conduct.

*Given Victoria's past,* I thought, *this stuff might prove useful one day.*

That day would come two months later.

You know it's winter in Chicago when the downtown law firms place their "Caution: Falling Ice!" signs in the middle of the sidewalks. In the weeks before Christmas, the Michigan Avenue tourists arrived in record numbers. Half of them wanted me to take their picture in front of the Wrigley Building. The other half took the pictures themselves—usually at the exact moment I was walking through.[103]

I expected some sort of emotional closure or logical conclusion from the semester's final lectures, but got nothing. "So this," I wanted Professor Ryder to say, "is the heart of civil procedure," followed by whatever the heart of civil procedure is. But civil procedure has no heart; constitutional law has no end point, and criminal law and contract law are continuously evolving doctrinal bodies; legislatures pass new statutes and judges create new precedents every single day. The closest thing I got to closure was the opportunity to fill out anonymous student evaluations and "grade" each of my professors, a very brief—and equally superficial—turning of

---

[103] Sorry!

the tables. Whereas the grades my professors gave me would determine my entire future, the grades I gave them would determine, as far as I could tell, absolutely nothing.

The evaluations asked us to rate our professors on a scale of 1 to 5 on such criteria as "Raises pertinent moral issues," and "Notes current developments in the law." They also had a section in which we were encouraged to write additional comments. Most students wrote nothing, but I felt obliged to compliment Laurel on his fairness, Dewey on her kindness, and Barry on his ability to keep me awake. On Devenpeck's evaluation, which, again, was anonymous, I wrote: "Perhaps you could stop every twenty or thirty minutes and ask us whether we are understanding everything," and, "You have my sincere congratulations on finding a Teaching Assistant even more condescending than you."

DePaul spaced out our exams over a two-week period. Professor Ryder's came first. She gave a five-question essay test to which we were permitted to bring a single 8½"×11" sheet of notes. Thus, our grades would be inversely proportional to the font size we could read.

I spent two days copying and pasting selected passages from my Civ Pro notes—I had 120 pages of them—into a separate word document that would eventually become my "cheat sheet." Using 6-point Times New Roman,[104] I was able to fit seventy-four hundred words onto a single sheet of paper.

Reading the words was difficult, but moving from the end

---

[104] Which looks like this.

of one line of text to the start of the next was impossible. A second sheet of paper used to underline the line of text I was reading would have helped, but, like I said, I was permitted to bring only one single sheet of paper to the exam. So here's what I did: at the end of the first line of text, I drew a blue dot. Then I drew a blue dot at the start of the second line. Then I drew a red dot at the end of the second line, and then a red dot at the start of the third, and then a green at the end of the third, and another green at the start of the fourth, and so on and so on. When I wanted to move from the end of one line to the start of the next, I just had to match the colors up.

I spent the night before the exam reading *Legalines,*[105] reviewing my class notes, and drinking gin. I asked my father and Victoria, who woke at seven every morning to commute downtown, where she worked in an upscale Michigan Avenue art gallery for wake-up calls. I set my alarm for 7:12 A.M., and got into bed around eleven.

I don't know who I was trying to fool; I wasn't tired at all.

At 11:30 P.M., I walked to Walgreens and bought a bottle of Advil PM. I took two and chased them with a glass of cheap port.[106] I was asleep by 12:15 A.M., the earliest I'd fallen asleep since elementary school.

---

[105] *Cliffs Notes* for law school.

[106] Before that night, I had never taken a sleeping pill in my life. Most of what I knew about over-the-counter drugs came from the infamous *Saved by the Bell* episode "Jessie's Song," in which Jessie overdosed on caffeine pills and sang/cried, "I'm so excited! I'm so excited! I'm so . . . *scared.*"

My phone rang at 7:11 A.M.

"Buongiorno, Principessa!"

"Buongiorno, Victoria. Mio sleepisimo. No dozo mucho."

"You're going to do great. Get out of bed, eat a good breakfast, and ace that thing."

After I hung up, the phone rang again. It was my dad.

"I'm so proud of you," he began.

"This really isn't the time."

"I know. I just want you to know how proud of you I am. I remember the morning of my first exam—"

"Really—it's too early for this."

"Okay, well, kick some ass."

It was the first and last time I ever heard my father say "ass."

I put on my only starched shirt and donned one of my pre-tied ties, set my iPod to Copland's *Appalachian Spring,* and wheeled my laptop and "cheat sheet"—by far the lightest load of the year—to the Lewis Center.

I found a seat and psyched myself up: *Look around you, Lax. These people want you to fail; the worse you do, the better they do. You're playing a zero-sum game, and you're playing to win. So kick some ass.*

I was ready. I had sat through over sixty hours of Civ Pro class and spent about two hundred studying the subject on my own time. I only missed two readings and I never missed a class.

The third-year student proctoring the exam handed out the nine-page test along with an instructional sheet for the exam software, explaining that if my laptop shut off suddenly during the exam, I should go to the front for a booklet and complete the rest of the exam by hand.

"Begin now."

I frantically flipped my exam over and read through the instructions. They were standard, but I had to read through them twice to pick that up; my anxiety overtook my concentration. And once I realized how anxious I was, well, that's when I got really anxious.

Ryder had warned us that the jurisdiction question would be long. But who could have imagined it would have been three pages?[107]

Harrah's Las Vegas, Inc., Harrah's Laughlin, Inc., Harrah's Operating Company, Inc. (HOC), Rio Properties, Inc., and Harvey's Tahoe Management Company, Inc. (collectively "the defendants") own and operate hotels in the state of Nevada. Frank Snow is a California resident. In 2001, plaintiff reserved a room by phone from his California residence at one of the hotels owned and operated by the defendants. To make the reservation, Snow gave the reservation agent his credit card number. At the time Snow made the reservation, the agent told him that the room would cost $50 per night plus the room tax. When Snow paid his bill at checkout, however, the bill included a $3 energy surcharge.

Snow filed the instant class action against the defendants and other entities on behalf of himself and other

---

[107] You'll probably want to skim this.

"persons who were charged an energy surcharge as an overnight hotel guest in one of the defendants' hotels, yet were never given notice that there was an energy surcharge and/or what such charge would be." In the complaint, Snow alleged that the defendants charged him and other guests an energy surcharge during their stays at hotels owned and operated by the defendants without providing notice of these charges during the reservation or check-in process. He further alleged that, in doing so, the defendants charged more than the advertised or quoted price. His complaint alleged causes of action for: (1) fraudulent and deceptive business practices in violation of Business and Professional Code; (2) breach of contract; (3) unjust enrichment; and (4) violations of Business and Professional Code.

In response, the defendants and other entities filed a motion to quash the summons for lack of personal jurisdiction. In support of the motion, the defendants submitted a declaration from Brad L. Kerby, the corporate secretary of HEI. Kerby stated that the defendants were incorporated in either Nevada or Delaware and maintained their principal place of business in Nevada. According to Kerby, the defendants conducted no business in California and had no bank accounts or employees in California. Kerby, however, acknowledged that HOC was licensed to do business in California and that Harrah's Marketing Services Corporation (HMSC), a wholly-owned subsidiary of HOC, operated offices in California to "assist customers who contact those offices" and "attempt[ed] to attract a limited number of high-end gaming patrons to Harrah's properties."

In opposition, Snow submitted several declarations, and transcript of Kerby's deposition, and various exhibits. This evidence established that the defendants: 1) advertised extensively to California residents through billboards in California, California newspapers, and California radio and television stations; 2) had a joint marketing agreement with National Airlines, which served Los Angeles and San Francisco, and advertised in the airline's print media; 3) maintained an interactive Web site that accepted reservations from California residents, provided driving directions to their hotels from California, and touted the proximity of their hotels to California; 4) accepted reservations from California residents through their Internet Web site and a toll-free phone number listed on the site and in their advertisements; 5) obtained a significant percentage of their patrons from California through reservations made through the toll-free number and Web site; and 6) regularly sent mailings to those California residents among the four to six million people enrolled in their "Total Rewards" program. Snow's evidence also confirmed that HMSC maintained several offices in California to handle reservations and market defendants' hotels.

The trial court granted the motion to quash for lack of personal jurisdiction. Specifically, the court found that Snow had failed to establish either general or specific jurisdiction. Snow appealed to the California Court of Appeals.

Assume you are a judge on the California Court of Appeals. Please write an opinion affirming or reversing the trial court. Set out your reason for doing so in detail.

*Do what?*

I freaked out. My heart began to race, my breathing quickened, and I hadn't even started. One student began typing. It was Bruce. *Did he actually read the entire problem and form an answer, or is this just an intimidation tactic?*

When I looked at the clock, I realized only 7 minutes had passed, leaving me 173. I hadn't lost much time at all. I took a deep breath, loosened my tie, and got to work.

First, I had to decide whether the trial court was right or wrong, and that was easy. They were wrong: "I reverse the opinion of the trial court; Snow made successful arguments for both general and specific jurisdiction."

Next, I entered a large portion of my "cheat sheet," verbatim:

In *International Shoe Co. v. Washington,* the court found that solicitation of orders for the purchase of goods within a state, to be accepted outside the state and filled by shipment of the purchased goods interstate, rendered a corporation amenable to suit within a state . . . *International Shoe* created a test that said you have to have minimum contacts with the forum state such that the maintenance of the suit does not offend traditional notions of fair play and substantial justice. In that case, the court found systematic and continuous contact.

And then I linked *International Shoe* with Snow's case:

I find systematic and continuous contact in the instant case. Snow's transcript of Kerby's depositions shows that the defendants advertised "extensively" to California residents through various media . . .

I spent the next hour and fifteen minutes listing all the ways Snow could get jurisdiction over the defendants.

The rest of the time flew by. By the time I'd answered the fifth question, I had less than ten minutes to go back and check through my work, which was unfortunate because I rarely get through a typed sentence without inverting a few letters. The exam software showed that I had typed almost four thousand words in 180 minutes.

Walking out of the Lewis Center, I passed Bruce, who was leaning against the side of the building and smoking.

"How do you think you did?" I asked.

"Another day, another A," he replied.

*This kid takes psychological warfare to a whole new level.*

Victoria called around one. We had reached the point where we were talking on the phone every day. Still, I wouldn't say we were "serious" because we had never had the "relationship talk."

"Are we going to celebrate tonight?" she asked.

"I can't; I have to start on Crim Law."

"You said that test wasn't for another four days."

"Everybody else is partying tonight, and if I start studying, I can get the competitive edge."

"But I haven't seen you all week."

"I've been studying nonstop. I only get one shot at this."

"You only get one shot at this relationship, too."

"What does that mean?"

"I don't know. I just miss you—that's all."

"I miss you, too."

I wanted to tell Victoria Barry's line about the legal system being my girlfriend, but I decided this wasn't the best moment for it. Instead, I bought her a 550-piece jigsaw puzzle featuring a pink Cosmopolitan on a simple blue background, (1) to keep her thinking about me during exams and (2) to keep her busy.

I surprised Victoria by dropping by unannounced to give her the puzzle. I told her I planned to head to a nearby twenty-four-hour diner to study and she asked if she could come study with me.

"That doesn't sound like the best idea."

"Why not?"

"Because . . . your beauty would distract me?"

"Go."

She was pissed. Maybe we *were* getting serious.

Before law school finals, I had never been addicted to any substance. While studying for Barry's Crim Law final, I realized I'd become addicted to two. I couldn't sleep without pills and couldn't breathe without nasal spray.

I thought Barry's closed-book 125-question multiple-choice exam went well. I can memorize a full deck of randomly shuffled playing cards in under five minutes, so, by comparison, memorizing the elements of common law burglary wasn't too difficult.[108]

After the exam, Victoria called again.

"Is this some sort of cruel joke?" she asked.

"What?"

"The puzzle, it's impossible. Every piece looks the exact same. They're all the exact same shade of blue. Come help me do it. Just for an hour."

"You know I want to—"

"Just an hour."

"I can't."

"Please."

"Okay."

When I arrived at Victoria's place I saw that in three days she and her roommate had only managed to assemble the puzzle's frame.

"It's hopeless," Victoria said.

"It can't be that hard."

"Tell you what: you put six pieces together and then you can go study."

"Do the six all have to connect with each other?"

---

[108] Breaking and entering a dwelling in the nighttime with the intent to commit a crime.

"Nope. Just make six connections and you can go study."

"That sounds fair."

It wasn't. I left Victoria's apartment after two hours having connected only five. By the time I'd settled down to study in the diner, it was already ten o'clock.

Laurel gave an open-book exam, with a liberal definition of "open-book": we were permitted to bring any book we wanted into the exam room, including commercial supplements like *Legalines*. "But I'd think twice," Laurel had advised, "before bringing a lot of materials into the exam. There is such a thing as having too much information at one's disposal. You don't want to spend the entire three hours searching through books."

Many of my classmates disregarded Laurel's advice and brought their Con Law casebooks, class notes, case briefs, outlines, and purchased supplements into the exam room. I only brought my *Legalines* supplement with me. I knew I could copy prewritten paragraphs into the exam software, like I had done for the Civ Pro test. *Legalines'* passages, I recognized, would work perfectly.

Laurel's questions weren't nearly as long as Ryder's. One of the questions had a fact pattern featuring a fictional multi-state slaughterhouse owner named Gregor Samsa.

"The Commerce Clause," I wrote, "went through a metamorphosis during FDR's presidency," hoping Laurel might give me a bonus point for catching his Kafka allusion and running with it.

When the exam ended, I thought I'd done well. Real

well. I didn't want to jinx my grade, but as the exam came to an end I couldn't help but think, *If anybody did better than me on this exam, I'd feel comfortable having them defend me in court were I to be framed for murder.*

*I probably shouldn't jinx that, either.*

Things didn't go so well for Cassandra: "I failed that exam," she said, waiting in line to sign out.

It was the first time Cassandra had initiated a conversation with me and, what's more, she had come to me for emotional support.

"You didn't fail the exam," I told her, knowing I couldn't be held legally accountable if she did.[109]

"I know I failed."

"It was a tough exam—that's all. It was equally tough for everybody."

"You don't understand: I failed. Ryder's exam was hard, too, but when I walked out of that one, I knew I did well."

I felt bad for her, but I looked forward to the effect her allegedly terrible performance might have on the curve.

"I just don't get it," she said. "I studied so hard—even on the weekends!"

"It's only one test. And you've got another chance to—"

"*Every* weekend."

It became clear that nothing I could say was going to calm Cassandra down. So I tried giving her a hug. She hugged back and didn't let go until well after I did.

Then I got my call from Victoria.

---

[109] An illusory promise.

"I like you more than the puzzle."

"That's reassuring. How's it coming, by the way?"

"We stayed up until two last night working on it."

"And?"

"We only got about thirty pieces connected."

"I have something to tell you," I said. "When I was at your place, I . . . I stole one of the pieces, as a prank, and then I lost it. I feel bad, and that's why I'm telling you about it now."

There was a pause at the other end of the line.

"You're lying," Victoria said.

"I'm not."

"You are."

"Okay, I am, but it'd be pretty funny if I wasn't."

"No, it wouldn't."

Marathon runners claim they get bursts of energy during the last miles of their races, and I had hoped something similar would happen to me while studying for Dewey's Contract exam.

No such luck.

But Dewey's exam, I realized, wasn't really my last; it was merely the last exam of my first semester. I wasn't almost done; I was almost one-sixth done. It was tough to get too excited about that.

Professor Dewey gave a multiple-choice test for which we were permitted to bring a self-annotated copy of the Uniform Commercial Code. We were allowed to fill every blank space of the UCC with notes, as long as we wrote them by hand. I spent three days copying my printed notes—115 pages' worth—by hand into the supplement.

I completed Dewey's exam in ninety-five minutes and spent the final eighty-five checking my work. In Crim Law, I had changed one of my answers; in Contract Law, I changed eight, then I changed some of them back, remembering something I'd learned while studying for the LSAT: in multiple-choice exams, first instincts are usually the best.

Then I changed two of the rechanged answers once again. If the exam had been longer, I'm sure I would have continued changing my answers until I passed out. That didn't happen; the third-year proctor called, "Time."

# CHAPTER FIVE

## Wild Unprofessionalism

"I remember you. Victoria—right?"

"Wait. Don't tell me. You look really familiar."

"Starts with an *R*. . . ."

"Rick! Ricky and Vicky! I remember. But it can't be you; you look so much older."

"Law school does that to you."

I took Victoria out for tapas and sangria, then to a trendy West Loop lounge for mojitos. Victoria wore tight black pants, black stilettos, and a copper corset top; having no clean laundry left, I wore a wrinkled dress shirt and wrinkled pants. With red eyes and an unshaven face, I looked like, well, a first-year law student who had just finished finals. I sensed everybody in the bar looking at Victoria with me and whispering, "He must be rich—probably a drug dealer or something."

Victoria's gallery gave her a week off, and we spent nearly every minute of it together, making up for lost time. Being an only child, I had always assumed I would kill anybody I spent that much time with, but Victoria made it through the week unscathed, and that's how I knew I really cared for her. During the week, we had all sorts of adventures, none of which involved illegal substances. We attended a hipster party at the Museum of Contemporary Art. We toured the Field Museum—the only natural history museum where the displays are older than the relics inside them. We barhopped our way from Wicker Park to Lincoln Park. We never did have the "relationship talk," but I sensed that we loved each other and were both just too chicken to say so.

One night we attended a Section 2 all-you-can-drink-a-thon at a bar called John Barleycorn. During finals, my classmates said they looked forward to a break from thinking about and talking about law school, but at John Barleycorn that's all they did. For a few minutes, Bruce indulged Victoria by asking her about twentieth-century art, but when Kimberly joined the conversation, she shifted the topic to the Sotheby's price-fixing scandal and then to criminal conspiracy and then, before I knew it, she was ranting about how white-collar criminals get such short sentences.

During the second week of break, I headed back home to Michigan, where my parents' questions never stopped: "How did finals go?" ("Well, I think.") "What makes you think that?" ("I just have a good feeling about it.") "What grades do you think you got?" ("That depends on how well my classmates did.") "How well do you think your classmates did?" ("Objection: speculation.") "Would you consider working at Maddin, Hauser?" ("Thanks, but no.") Most of my classmates would happily take a job at a firm like my father's, but if I always had my father around to answer my legal questions, double-check my memorandums, and tie my ties, I'd never do any legal research, double-checking, or tie tying on my own. I'd never grow up. Taking up my father's profession was one thing; working at his office would be another—it'd be one step away from marrying my mom.

Over break, my father and I threw phrases like "bargained-for consideration" and "promissory estoppel" around the dinner table and my poor mother just sat there, playing with her food and wondering what had happened to our family's nonlawyer majority.

Within two days of arriving home, I'd resumed my *Price Is Right*–watching habits, but not my *Price Is Right*–watching mind-set. Something felt different. I suddenly felt guilty abusing my parents' resources and providing nothing but legalese in return.

So I went on the road with Tally Hall, whose song "Banana Man" had just been featured on the seventeenth season of MTV's *The Real World*.[110] I made myself useful by selling T-shirts and CDs at concession stands, lugging amplifiers on and off the band's van, and performing card tricks for Tally Hall's fans, who, since the band's song had appeared on MTV, had gotten younger and younger.

Like the Tally Hall guys, I wore a shirt and tie most nights, so teenage girls were constantly coming up to me and asking for my autograph, assuming that I was in the band. And who was I to disappoint them? I never directly lied to these girls, but I didn't volunteer information, either:

"I'm like your biggest fan."

[110] One of the housemates was nicknamed "Johnny Banana," so MTV played the song whenever he was on-screen.

"*Really?* Thanks."

Sometimes I came off as a cocky jerk:

"Tally Hall is my favorite band!"

"Mine, too!"

And other times, just odd:

"You were awesome tonight."

"You were pretty good yourself."

One girl in New Jersey had me sign her T-shirt and then her CD and then she said, "Wait . . . which instrument do you play again?"

After the New Jersey gig, Victoria called and asked, "Where the *fuck* is it?"

"Where's what?"

"Don't play dumb; just tell me where it is."

"I don't know what—"

"You took a puzzle piece."

"I was joking about that."

In my absence, Victoria and her roommate had completed all but one piece of the puzzle.

"It's probably under the sofa or behind the cushions."

"We looked there. We looked everywhere. It's not here. And you were the only person besides us who worked on it."

"You must have had other people in your apartment the past few weeks."

"Those people didn't work on the puzzle, and none of them would do anything like this."

"That's pure speculation."

"Don't talk lawyer to me. Just tell me where the damn piece is."

I'm not above stealing a puzzle piece as a joke, and I didn't claim that I was; I just reiterated that I had not taken the piece. Victoria didn't believe me, and I doubt a jury of twelve of my peers would have, either.

Even if I had taken the puzzle piece, *which I hadn't,* it wouldn't have been that mean of a prank—right? It was just a stupid puzzle—right?

"This is about more than just a stupid puzzle. Do you have any idea how long I've spent working on this? I've been doing it nonstop. I could kill you right now."

"By the time I get back to Chicago, you'll have forgotten about the puzzle and you'll just be happy to see me."

"Fuck you."

Click.

DePaul posted our grades the week before second-semester classes began. In college, I'd always had a pretty good idea of what my grades would be before I got them. I didn't know I was going to fail my fourth semester of Italian, but I'd had a pretty good idea that I wasn't going to get an A, given that I didn't speak Italian. The only first-semester law school grade I could estimate was my Legal Writing grade; I had received above-average grades on all my assignments, so I figured I'd get a B+ at the least.

I logged onto law.depaul.edu, entered the "Students Only" section, and clicked on "Grades." Here's what I saw:

Contract Law:    B
Criminal Law:    B+

| | |
|---|---|
| Civil Procedure: | B+ |
| Constitutional Law: | A |
| Legal Writing: | B |
| GPA: | 3.469 |

A 3.469 GPA put me at the twentieth percentile, meaning (1) that I probably wouldn't be defending indigent baby rapists, after all, (2) that I could afford my future trophy wife's pet psychic's bills, and (3) that unless I completely fell off the legal deep end during my second semester, I would hold on to my scholarship. That was the good news.

The bad news was that I had only received a B in Legal Writing, which made no mathematical sense.

I knocked on Devenpeck's door. No answer.

I knew he was in his office because I heard him typing, so I waited fifteen seconds and knocked again.

"Yes?"

When I opened the door, Devenpeck was holding a plate of salad.

"I'm eating lunch."

I deduced that he had just picked up said salad before opening the door.

"Should I come back later?"

"You *can* come back later."

"When are you done with lunch?"

"Later."

I waited two hours and then returned. Devenpeck's door was open. He was sitting behind a mountain of paperwork and a still-full plate of wilted salad.

"Well?" Devenpeck asked.

"I wanted to talk about my grade—"

"Look at my desk. I have to do all this in the next two days."

"So should I come back after that?"

"Remind me to have a 'can'/'may'/'should' lesson in class next week."

"Maybe you could give me my graded memo in the meantime so I can look through it to prepare for our meeting? I must have bombed it, because all of my grades have been above average, and—"

"I can't give you your memo right now."

"I thought you said we'd get them back."

"I'm not giving you your memo," Devenpeck said, nodding at his file cabinet as if to indicate the memo would only take a minute to retrieve, "until I'm ready to give it back to you."

I should have walked out at that point, but instead I said this: "Real quick: All my grades were above average, but I got a B and I just wanted to know why. I mean, unless I absolutely bombed the final memo, I—"

"Mr. Lax, you have my sincere congratulations on telling me the absolute least of my concerns. Among other things, I have two scheduled meetings, the first of which was supposed to begin five minutes ago, so I will see you in a few days."

Had Devenpeck recognized my handwriting on the evaluation form: "You have my sincere congratulations on finding a Teaching Assistant even more condescending than you"? Devenpeck had seen my memorably poor handwriting while grading my legal research workbook assignment, and he must have known that assignment was mine . . . *because it didn't have answers to questions 4 through 8.*

Walking down the eighth-floor hallway, I passed Cassandra, who was no longer wearing her trademark crucifix necklace or bracelet.

"How was break?" I asked.

"Awful."

"Is everything okay?"

"No."

I didn't set out to eavesdrop on Cassandra and Devenpeck's meeting[111] but I couldn't help but overhear snippets as I chatted with Adrienne, who had arrived moments after Cassandra walked into Devenpeck's office.

"You meeting with Devenpeck, too?" Adrienne asked.

"I tried to, but I guess not. You?"

"Yeah, we're supposed to go over my grade."

My conversation with Adrienne continued as we half-listened in on Cassandra's meeting. As far as I could tell, Cassandra, who had never gotten anything below a B since middle school, had gotten a B− in Civ Pro, a C in Con Law, and a C in Legal Writing.

Cassandra's meeting ended abruptly, and when she walked out of Devenpeck's office, she caught Adrienne and me listening in. Cassandra hid her face beneath her forearm, but it was too late: we'd already seen her tears. Cassandra charged past us.

---

[111] *Mens rea* ≠ intent.

"Hope my meeting goes better than that," Adrienne said.

Marty got a B+ in Crim Law. If Barry was serious about lowering Marty's grade half a point for his in-class unpreparedness, Marty must have scored an A on the exam. In fact, Marty got As in Contracts, Civ Pro, and Legal Writing—the bastard.

"We did awesome," he said. "Maybe we'll get those Kirkland and Ellis jobs after all."

"*You* might; *I'm* not in the top ten percent."

"Fuck that; you did awesome. We're going to celebrate."

"Where?"

"Everybody's heading to McFadden's."

I swear they were playing Bon Jovi's "Living on a Prayer" when we walked in. I found Section 2 in the VIP room doing shots. Cassandra was there and doing shots like everyone else. She had not only started drinking; she had adopted Erik's one-drink-per-hand technique. I found her leaning against the wall—for support, not to look cool.

"Don't you have to wake up for church tomorrow morning?"

"I CAN'T HEAR YOU."

"I SAID, 'DON'T YOU HAVE TO WAKE UP FOR CHURCH TOMORROW MORNING?'"

"I'M SKIPPING. DON'T TELL JESUS, OKAY?"

"OKAY. I WON'T TELL HIM ABOUT YOUR GETTING DRUNK, EITHER."

"DRINKING IS FUN."

"YOU JUST GOT THE MEMO?"

"HA-HA."

*Finally, somebody who appreciates memo humor.*

"WHAT HAPPENED TO YOUR NECKLACE AND BRACELET?"

"I LOST THEM OVER BREAK. WHAT DID YOU LOSE OVER BREAK? YOUR VIRGINITY?"

This was the first "joke" Cassandra had ever told me, and maybe the first joke she had ever told, period, so like a mother putting her four-year-old son's first finger painting on the refrigerator door, I managed a laugh.

Cassandra's bracelet and necklace weren't the only things she had lost over break; she had also lost the majority of her skirt. Cassandra had worn ankle-length skirts to school nearly every day—there were three of them, in rotation—but that night in the middle of January she was sporting half of a miniskirt.

She had also lost her inhibitions and was falling all over me. While that sounds sexy on paper, in practice it wasn't.

"I GOT A TWO POINT SIX," SHE SAID.

"I KNOW"—OOPS—"WHAT YOU MEAN." *Nice.* "LAW SCHOOL'S TOUGHER THAN I THOUGHT."

"HOW'D YOU DO?" she asked.

"I DID OKAY."

"COME ON, TELL ME HOW YOU DID."

"NOT AS GOOD AS I HAD HOPED."

I couldn't tell Cassandra that I scored almost a full point better than her, so I tried to play it off like my GPA was so bad that I was too embarrassed to share it. It didn't work.

"YOU'RE REALLY GOOD AT DODGING QUES-TIONS," Cassandra said. "YOU'RE GOING TO MAKE A

REALLY GOOD LAWYER AND YOU PROBABLY DID REALLY WELL, SO JUST TELL ME WHAT YOU GOT."

I attempted a topic change: "SO WHEN DID YOU START DRINKING?"

"THREE HOURS AGO."

"NO, I MEAN, YOU DIDN'T DRINK, AND NOW YOU DO. WHEN DID YOU START?"

"WHY DO YOU CARE?"

"JUST CURIOUS."

"WHY? ARE YOU MY FATHER?"

*I'm not going down that road.*

"NEVER MIND."

"FINE, I'LL TELL YOU: I STARTED AFTER WE GOT OUR GRADES BACK."

According to Illinois's Lawyers' Assistance Program (LAP), an organization formed to assist lawyers and law students with alcohol and drug dependency problems, 30 percent of law students admit to abusing alcohol during law school. The remaining 70 percent probably suspect, as I do, that the LAP is just a front for the Committee on Character and Fitness, always looking to weed out the alcoholics. Like Cassandra, more than one-third of the admittedly alcohol-abusing law students report that they began abusing alcohol during law school. *Student Lawyer* contributor Cynthia L. Cooper says that law students' alcohol abuse doesn't end upon graduation:

> During the last decade, the legal profession began facing up to a crisis of chemical dependency problems. Studies indicate that lawyers engage in higher-than-average

drug and alcohol abuse, affecting from 15 percent to 18 percent of the profession, compared with 10 percent of the general population.

Disciplinary bodies discover that chemical dependency problems are at the root of 40 percent to 70 percent of complaints about lawyers . . .

If Cassandra and Erik and the rest of the Section 2 students were any indication, lawyers' drug and alcohol dependency problems begin during the first year of law school. Students like Cassandra drank to dull their defeats, students like Marty drank to celebrate their victories, and all of us drank to cope with the stress. The more stressed we got, the more we drank. And my stress was only beginning.

When classes began, Room 815's front and back rows were empty. I don't know how many students dropped out of Section 2 after first semester,[112] but I do know that three students dropped out of my Legal Writing group alone, including Bruce, who had returned to L.A. to work for his aunt and pay off his student loans.

I told him to call me when he wound up in jail.

I took a seat between Marty and a muscular guy with a crew cut who always wore sweatpants to class. During first semester, we'd had several conversations about online poker— he played during class, for money—only I'd never actually

[112] And the Family Education Rights and Privacy Act prevents the DePaul University College of Law faculty from sharing this information with me.

learned his name. And because an entire semester had passed, it was too late to say, "By the way, I never learned your name," so I just called him "man" "buddy." Anyway, Manbuddy was sitting next to another muscular guy, and their conversation went like this:

"How was break?"

"Not long enough."

"What'd you do?"

"Tried to remember why I wanted to come here in the first place. You?"

"Thought about killing myself."

They were no less excited to be back than the two blond girls sitting behind me:

"Ready for round two?"

"Fucking shoot me. I can't take another semester of this shit."

I began to suspect that I was the only person in Section 2 who was actually enjoying law school—not Legal Writing, but the rest of it. I asked Marty, "Do you hate law school?"

"I tolerate it quite well, actually. How about you?"

"I kind of like it," I said.

Marty felt my forehead with the back of his hand.

Nobody says they like law school. Eighty-five percent of students hate it and the 15 percent who like it say they hate it too because saying otherwise raises eyebrows. The only time students say they like law school is during interviews, because, once again, saying otherwise raises eyebrows.

Torts professor Samuel Isaac looked like a stereotypical lawyer. He showed up wearing a light gray suit and a dark red tie held in place by a thick silver tie clip. He had slicked-back gray hair and wire-rimmed glasses. The Section 2 professors had generally kept their personal political leanings to themselves, but not Isaac: "First day of a new semester, President Bush's approval rating is at an all-time low, and last night my wife and I had twelfth-row seats to see Barbra Streisand—which, by the way, put me back five hundred and fifty dollars—so I'm in heaven right now. How are all of you? Good? Good.

"What is a tort?" asked Isaac. "A tort is a wrong for which the law provides a remedy. There are two kinds of torts: intentional and unintentional. An intentional tort is when you punch somebody (that's called 'battery') or when you hurt somebody's feelings (that's called 'intentional infliction of emotional distress' and we'll discuss it in a moment) or when you kill somebody (which, in tort law, is called 'wrongful death'). Unintentional torts happen when you forget to salt your driveway and somebody slips and falls on it or when you crash your car into a pedestrian or when you brew your coffee too hot and an old lady spills a cup of it on herself. When those things happen, we say that you acted 'negligently' and then we sue you, and we settle, and then nobody is happy, and that's how we know we've reached a good settlement."

Isaac had assigned us *Slocum v. Food Fair Stores of Florida,* an intentional tort case in which grocery store shopper Julia Slocum asked a Food Fair worker how much a particular item cost and the worker replied, "If you want to know the price, you'll have to find out the best way you can. You stink to me." In response, Slocum had a heart attack.[113] She sued Food Fair Stores of Florida for "mental suffering or emotional distress, and an ensuing heart attack and aggravation of pre-existing heart disease." The court sided with Food Fair Stores:

> The courts have from an early date granted relief for offense reasonably suffered by a patron from insult by a servant or employee of a carrier, hotel, theater, and most recently, a telegraph office . . . a line of demarcation should be drawn between conduct likely to cause mere "emotional distress" and that causing "severe emotional distress" so as to exclude the situation at bar.

Isaac paced up and down 815's center aisle as he explained the judge's reasoning.

"The court used an objective test in determining whether the insult was calculated to cause significant emotional distress. Telling somebody they 'stink' isn't the nicest thing you could say to them, but people say meaner things to me on the L every morning."

To recover for intentional infliction of emotional distress, you need to show the statement was intentional or reckless,

113

that it was extreme and outrageous, that it caused the distress, and that the distress was severe. The Food Fair worker's statement was intentional, but, as Isaac pointed out it wasn't extreme and it wasn't outrageous; "You stink to me" is one of the most polite insults I've ever heard, falling somewhere between "you deeply displease me" and "what an unpleasant fellow you are!"

After Torts, I stopped by Devenpeck's office and he returned my memo. I hadn't bombed it; my grade was above the class average.

"How did I consistently get above-average grades on my assignments but just a B in the class? I don't understand the math. I mean, my overall grade is based on my individual assignment grades—right?"

"The formula I use to construct my grades is privileged information. It falls under the work-product doctrine."

"Can you tell me how close I was to getting a B-plus?"

"That information also falls under the work-product doctrine."

"Can you at least tell me if you use the grading curve set out in the Student Handbook?"

"My grading curve is confidential information. If I tell you the curve, you might figure out what grades other students received."

"How would I do that?"

Devenpeck sighed and said, "Mr. Lax, may I be frank with you? This conversation is wildly unprofessional. Your line of questioning doesn't reflect well on you as a future attorney or as a person."

I went straight to the Dean of Internal Affairs' office to find out whether everything Devenpeck had just told me was true.

The Dean of Internal Affairs said, "Here's how it is: I've never seen a single grade-change petition granted, but you can try if you'd like."

"I just want to understand how I got the grade I got. I got above-average grades on all my assignments, but only a B in the class, and Professor Devenpeck said he wasn't allowed to tell me how close I was to getting a B-plus or tell me how many students got what grades. He said that telling me that stuff would violate the work-product doctrine and that—"

"He's wrong."

"He's wrong?"

"He's wrong. He can tell you. Was that all?"

"Wait—he *can* tell me or he *has to* tell me?"

"He doesn't *have* to tell you anything, and I'm guessing he doesn't want to tell you anything."

I wanted to march back to Devenpeck's office and say, "You were *wrong*. The Dean of Internal Affairs just told me so." But then Devenpeck would ask how, specifically, he was wrong and then I would have to tell him that he was *allowed* to tell me how close I was to getting a B-plus and how many students got what grades and then he would say, "Well, Mr. Lax, if I am permitted but not required to share that information with you, then I choose not to share it." Another reason not to tell Devenpeck that he was wrong was that I had to deal with him for another semester. So I did my best to forget about the whole matter and went to Barnes & Noble to do my first Property reading—a fifty-five pager.

My textbook, *Property* by Jesse Dukeminier and James E. Krier, claimed to "trace in broad outline the development of property law, emphasizing that part of history still important in understanding modern concepts," and then it recounted the following story:

> In January 1066, Edward the Confessor, saintly and celibate, died childless. Three contenders claimed the English crown: Harold Godwinson, the most powerful earl in England, who had been granted the kingdom by Edward on his deathbed; Harald Hardrade, king of Norway, an adventurer assisted by Harold Godwinson's exiled brother Tostig; and William of Normandy, Edward's cousin . . . Harold Godwinson was crowned king, defeated Harald of Norway in September, and on October 14 was himself defeated by William of Normandy in the battle of Hastings on the south coast of England. This fateful event—the conquest of England by the Normans from across the channel—determined the whole future course of English, and consequently American, law.

I couldn't see how that convoluted story was important to understanding modern property law concepts, and I looked forward to Professor Holmes's explanation. I was tempted to skim through the rest, but I feared being caught unprepared, so I read every word.

Miriam Holmes had been teaching at DePaul for three

decades, and her teaching style could best be described as one part quiet, two parts dull. On the plus side, she seemed easy: "I don't like the Socratic Method. I'm not saying I won't call on any of you; I'm just saying I don't plan to. But even if I do, and even if you're unprepared, it's no big deal. If you have something to say, just raise your hand and say it. If I need a question answered, I'll ask for a volunteer. The one thing I ask is that you all try to volunteer at least once before the semester is over."

Some students only did their readings because they were afraid of getting called on, and Holmes had just told those students, in so many words, that there would be no assigned readings in Property.

"I'm not sure how many of you actually did that awful assigned reading, but for those of you who did, good for you. I'm not sure how useful it will be in this class or on my exam, but if you did read it then, yes, good for you."

*Good for me?* I had spent over three hours doing that damn reading. Had it all been for nothing? Had I learned that, until 1536, the only way to transfer a freehold estate was through a *feoffment* with *livery of seisin,*[114] for nothing? If Holmes thought the reading was so "awful," then why did she assign it?

"We'll go over next class's reading carefully, though"— *sure we will*—"so spend some time on it. I'm going to let you out early today, but before I do, I want to tell you that there

[114] *Livery of seisin:* a ceremony in which one person hands a clod of dirt over to another and says, "Know ye that I have given this land to you."

will be a midterm in this class. I understand your section didn't have any last semester, so I just want you all to be ready for it."

In Contracts, Dewey taught us *Webb v. McGowin,* which involved two W. T. Smith Lumber Company workers, one of whom was clearing the mill's upper floor of seventy-five-pound pine blocks:

> As [Joe Webb] started to turn the block loose so that it would drop to the ground, he saw J. Greeley McGowin . . . on the ground below and directly under where the block would have fallen had [Webb] turned it loose . . . The only safe and reasonable way to prevent this was for [Webb] to hold to the block and divert its direction in falling from the place where McGowin was standing and the only safe way to divert it so as to prevent its coming into contact with McGowin was for [Webb] to fall with it to the ground below. [Webb] did this, and by holding to the block and falling with it to the ground below . . . He was badly crippled for life and rendered unable to do physical or mental labor.

McGowin agreed to pay Webb fifteen dollars, every two weeks, for the rest of Webb's life, but after McGowin died, his estate refused to continue the payments and Webb sued. The court held that because Webb had saved McGowin "from death or grievous bodily harm, and McGowin subsequently agreed to pay him," Webb had made a valid and enforceable contract.

Dewey contrasted that case with *Mills v. Wyman*. Levi Wyman had just returned deathly ill from a voyage at sea. Daniel Mills took care of him for two weeks, until Wyman's death, without being asked. Wyman's father wrote Mills and promised to pay him for his services. He never paid, and Mills sued. The court found that "[T]he kindness and services towards [Levi Wyman] were not bestowed at his request . . . [Daniel Mills] acted the part of the Good Samaritan, giving him shelter and comfort until he died." The court gave Mills nothing.

The moral of the two cases was clear: don't do favors for people unless you plan to maim yourself in the process. That lesson was totally lost on the half of my classmates who had stopped paying attention in class—to Professor Dewey, not to Spider Solitaire or perezhilton.com. The lesson was partially lost on me; I'd been checking my e-mail during class and discovered that the dean of Internal Affairs had sent a copy of the Dean's List to the entire section. By the end of class, most students knew who'd made the list and who hadn't—and I had. What my classmates didn't know was that making the list was probably the most impressive achievement of my academic career.[115]

Marty and Kimberly had made the Dean's List, too. Dan and most of the serious students had made the list . . . but

---

[115] I say "probably" because my most impressive academic accomplishment might have been a paper I wrote for Mrs. Martin's AP English class about playwright Peter Shaffer's two major works, *Amadeus* and *Equus*, which I titled "Mediocrity and Horsef#*k!ng." I got an A on that paper. It was the only A I got in that class all year.

not Nadeeka. Finding my name on the list was no more exciting than finding Nadeeka's absent. Not finding Nadeeka's name on the Dean's List was surprising but not as surprising as finding Erik's name on it. Was Erik a genius or did he study more than he let on? Did he consciously cultivate the study-free frat boy image to put Section 2 at false academic ease, thus giving him the competitive advantage? Did he really drink as much as he claimed? After class, I found Erik in the seventh-floor student lounge and congratulated him on making the list.

"Out of curiosity," I said, "how much do you really study?"

"The funny thing is, when I slept with the dean, I didn't even know he had a list," Erik joked. He wasn't about to reveal his secrets to me.

I called Victoria. I wanted to tell her about my achievement and that my putting her on the back burner hadn't been for nothing. But I couldn't figure out a polite way to say it, so I just said that we should meet in person to discuss the missing puzzle piece. She reluctantly agreed to presume me innocent until proven guilty. She agreed to meet at the Water Tower Place mall, because, as she put it, "Being in a public place will keep me from doing anything too violent to you."

When Victoria saw me, she grabbed my collar with both hands, pulled me in, and gave me a kiss.

I didn't think Victoria had forgotten about the puzzle piece, but if she had, I wasn't about to bring it up.

"About the puzzle piece"—*damn*—"I honestly think that you took it, but maybe you didn't, and maybe I was wrong to get so mad at you. Even if you did take it, it's just a puzzle piece. No big deal."

That sounded suspicious.

"Really?" I asked.

"Really. And if you did take it, at this point, I'd take it back from you, no questions asked."

Suspicious indeed; Victoria hadn't forgotten anything; she was looking for a confession and wasn't above using a dramatic kiss to loosen my lips.

"Victoria." I put on my serious lawyer face. "I don't have your puzzle piece."

She watched my eyes, thought for a moment, and then said, "I believe you."

And I believed that she believed me.

"You look good," Victoria said.

"You'd be surprised what not studying nine hours a day does for your complexion."

"You look ten years younger—easily."

"I feel like a thirteen-year-old, too."

"We should get you some candy."

Victoria led me by the hand to a nearby chocolate shop to score some free samples. But when we got there, there were none.

"What happened to the free samples?" Victoria asked the "Master Chocolatier" behind the counter.

"We don't do that anymore," the Chocolatier replied, to Victoria's chest.

She put on her sexiest expression and asked, "Do you think you could make an exception for me?"

The Chocolatier looked from Victoria's chest to me, then back to Victoria.

"Sorry, no."

Victoria walked to the back of store. The Chocolatier looked from her butt, to me, and then back to her butt, as if to say, "I'll look at your girl's ass if I want to. You're on the candy man's turf now."

Victoria reached into a chest of individually wrapped truffles, pulled out a handful, and stuffed them into her purse. I didn't know whether she hoped the Chocolatier wouldn't see or whether this was meant as an open act of defiance.

A few accomplice liability cases flashed before my eyes. In one, a guy was convicted for watching a crime "without disapproving or opposing." In another, lending one's "countenance and approval" to a crime counted as aiding and abetting. In a third, the judge said that "hitting on" somebody made you their accomplice.

I was looking guilty no matter how you sliced it.

But the Chocolatier, suddenly, wasn't watching my girlfriend. Maybe he had seen Victoria put the truffles in her purse and was merely pretending he hadn't because he didn't want to start a fight or because he was planning to wait until we left the store to call security.

As Victoria made for the door, I remembered that the one way to get out of accomplice liability was to withdraw from the crime. I remembered that a withdrawal would only be effective if (1) I terminated my conduct before the offense was committed and (2) I neutralized the effects of my conduct. Technically, Victoria hadn't yet committed the crime of theft; she hadn't walked out of the store yet. There was still time.

"Victoria," I said, but she kept walking. So I said her name again, a little louder, but she kept walking. So I grabbed her by the shoulder and said, "You have to check this thing out!"

I walked her back to the truffle chest.

"Do you have any idea what the penalty for shoplifting is?"

"You're supposed to be my boyfriend, not my lawyer."

"As your boyfriend, I say this to you: Put the chocolates back. Please. Just put them back."

She looked angry and then resigned. She put them back and we left the shop.

"Shoplift often?"

"Not anymore."

"Let me guess: you stopped when you stopped dealing drugs?"

"No. I haven't dealt drugs for years. I stole these heels from Nordstrom three months ago."

"So you do still shoplift."

"Not really. I could see how upset you were about the drugs, and I've been looking for an excuse to quit breaking the law, so I figured you could be my catalyst. These shoes were the last thing I took."

"So what happened back there?"

"The guy behind the counter was being a dick and I just snapped, I guess."

Victoria wasn't the first shoplifter I knew. My magic camp counselor moonlighted as a professional shoplifter. Retail stores hired him to test their security staffs. Shoplifting and performing magic have a lot in common: both require hand/eye coordination, nerves of steel, and the ability to make the difficult look easy.[116] The magician in me wanted to help Victoria,[117] but the future attorney in me

---

[116] Close-up magician Michael Ammar, who is *not* a shoplifter, bridged the fields of shoplifting and magic when he turned the shoplifter's Poacher's Pouch (a black bag safety-pinned to the outside of a shirt and the inside of a jacket) into the safety-pin-free Topit, which stage magicians use to vanish playing cards, rubber balls, and wine bottles.

[117] The thing that would have helped Victoria most was the magician's principle of *justification*. Let's say I want to make a coin disappear. The simplest way to do that is to hold it in my right hand, pretend to place it in my left (magicians call that a *false transfer*), secretly drop the coin from my right hand into my right pant pocket (while staring at my left hand for misdirection), and then show my left hand empty. The hardest part of the trick isn't pretending to place the coin in my left hand; it's dropping the coin from my right hand into my right pocket without the spectator noticing. One way to get around this problem is to justify a deliberate reach into my right pocket (dropping off the coin in the process) by, say, pulling out a pen from my right pocket and using it to tap my left fist, as if the tap were a crucial part of the effect.

What was Victoria's justification for reaching into the chest of chocolates? What was her justification for reaching into her purse? She had none. She should have taken a handful of truffles out of the chest, walked toward the counter as if she were going to buy them, and then paused, as if she were having second thoughts. She should have then walked back to the chest and dumped most of the chocolates back, secretly palming the few she planned to steal. She should have then continued "browsing" for a minute and then reached into her purse, dropped off the chocolates, pulled out her cell phone, opened it up, and said, "You're here?! Already?! I'm on my way!" That would have justified her leaving the store posthaste.

knew the Committee on Character and Fitness wouldn't stand for it.[118]

"I'm sure you all missed me every bit as much as I missed you. And I'm sure you're every bit as happy to be back here as I am."

The second semester of Legal Writing had begun.

"It has come to my attention that one of you has been making complaints about the legal writing program. Formal complaints. Extremely unprofessional—that's all I can say for now."

*Had my brief meeting with the Dean of Internal Affairs constituted a "formal complaint"? No; somebody else must have said something.* Everybody looked around the room trying to figure out who had made the complaints. I was the most likely suspect, only it wasn't me—at least I didn't think it was.

"Two things will be different this semester. First, you will be permitted to do computerized legal research. I suggest setting up an appointment with a LexisNexis or Westlaw counselor to learn how to do this, because we won't be going over it in class. Second, I will be giving you your assignments orally, because that's how it's done in the real world. I suggest that you listen very carefully, because I don't plan to repeat myself."

Devenpeck gave us a new fact pattern involving a man named Samir Reddy, who worked at the Linque Botique.

[118] Model Rule of Professional Conduct 1.2 (d) says: "A lawyer shall not counsel a client to engage, or assist a client, in conduct that the lawyer knows is criminal or fraudulent."

After Reddy's personal assistant quit, Reddy began to miss important deadlines and the number of misspellings in his paperwork skyrocketed. Reddy's clients contacted Reddy's boss, Sushma Khaleel, about the missed deadlines and the errors, and Khaleel told Reddy to clean up his act. In response, Reddy revealed to Khaleel that he had ADHD and said that Linque Botique had a legal obligation, under the Americans with Disabilities Act, to hire him a replacement personal assistant.

Devenpeck split the class in two. Half of us would represent Linque Botique and would argue:

1. that Reddy was not "disabled" within the meaning of the Americans with Disabilities Act but merely opportunistic,
2. that Reddy was not "otherwise qualified" to perform an "essential function" of his job with or without "reasonable accommodation" (an ADA requirement), and
3. that Linque Botique, a small mom-and-pop operation, could not reasonably accommodate Reddy's request without incurring an undue financial burden.

The other half of the class would argue:

1. that Reddy was the exact type of worker the ADA was passed to protect,
2. that Reddy's request was reasonable, if not downright modest, and

3. that Linque Botique could easily spare the money from its $720,000-dollar-per-year operating budget to hire Reddy a new secretary.

"I hope you were listening carefully to all of that, because you're going to spend the entire semester with that fact pattern," Devenpeck said. "First you'll write an intraoffice memo—that's due in three weeks. Then you'll write a legal brief for the court, and then you'll give an oral argument on this case before a panel of three, composed of myself and two real judges."

Devenpeck gave us a legal notation assignment and let us go ten minutes late. Devenpeck and Kiki were the first ones out of the classroom, and after they left, I asked who had made the formal complaint.

"I did," Cassandra said. "I'll tell you about it after Torts."

Isaac reviewed what our textbook editors called "the great-grandparent of all assault cases," which took place in England in 1348: *I de S et ux.*[119] *v. W de S.*

W de S "beat upon the door with a hatchet." Though the hatchet didn't hit M (plaintiff I de S's wife), the court said, "there is harm done and a trespass for which [I de S] shall recover damages since [W de S] made an assault upon the woman, as has been found, although he did no other harm."

---

[119] *Et ux.:* short for the Latin *et uxor,* meaning "and the wife." Women weren't allowed to bring lawsuits in fourteenth-century England.

Fast-forward 585 years to *Western Union Telegraph Co. v. Hill,* in which plaintiff J. B. Hill's wife[120] came to Sapp, an agent of Western Union Telegraph Company, and asked him to fix her clock. Sapp, who was standing behind a counter, said, "If you will come back here and let me love and pet you, I will fix your clock." Sapp also tried to put his hand on her, and though he failed, the *Western Union* court said that to qualify as an assault there must only be "an intentional, unlawful, offer to touch the person of another in a rude or angry manner under such circumstances as to create in the mind of the party alleging the assault a well-founded fear of an imminent battery, coupled with the apparent present ability to effectuate the attempt, if not prevented."

After class, I found Cassandra and got the full "formal complaint" story. Two days after her meeting with Devenpeck, she'd gone to the Dean of Internal Affairs, just as I had, to talk about the legal writing program. Cassandra told the Dean of Internal Affairs that we didn't receive written feedback on our assignments until after the following assignments were due, making it impossible to incorporate the feedback, that there were large discrepancies in the materials given to the students in different sections, and that students felt that their questions and concerns weren't being adequately addressed.

"What did the dean tell you?"

"She seemed to be hinting that I was only complaining because I was mad about my grade."

[120] Apparently women weren't allowed to bring lawsuits in twentieth-century Alabama, either.

When Cassandra and I got to the elevator bank, we ran into Kiki, so Cassandra changed the topic: "Are you going to the Boat Cruise?"

"Indeed I am."

The one social event the entire class attended was the February Boat Cruise, a fifty-five-dollar, four-hour ride on the *Spirit of Chicago* that, according to the SBA brochure, featured a "breathtaking view of the city," a "disco ball dance floor," a "gourmet dinner buffet," and "all the alcohol you can drink."

"Do you want to go together?" Cassandra asked. "Let me give you my number."

*The one you refused to give me first semester?*

"Maybe we can meet up beforehand and get a taxi to Navy Pier together," she offered.

"Actually," I said, "I was planning on spending Saturday afternoon with my girlfriend."

The mind is a funny thing; as soon as Cassandra had become obtainable, she had become undesirable.

The *Spirit of Chicago* docks at Navy Pier. Tourists typically arrive at Navy Pier with digital cameras dangling round their necks and *Eyewitness* travel guides tucked under their arms, and when they see the pier's parks, gardens, funhouse, IMAX theater, and 150-foot Ferris wheel, they usually say, "Too touristy. Let's go to the Sears Tower."

Victoria and I spent Saturday afternoon touring Navy Pier, pretending to be newlywed Czech tourists on our honeymoon. At six, we boarded the ship, which resembled a floating bar mitzvah party. As is often the case with open-bar events, there were too few bartenders. By seven, some of my classmates began ordering drinks by the twos and threes, which made the lines even longer, so to justify the additional wait, the rest of my classmates started ordering drinks by the twos and threes, too.

The captain's voice came over the loudspeaker: "I've got some bad news: due to extreme winds and an incoming thunderstorm, we're going to have to dock back at Navy Pier."

"This is a total contract violation," I told Cassandra. "I was promised a 'breathtaking view of the city.' This frustrates the purpose of the whole cruise."

"The purpose of the cruise," Cassandra replied, "is to get plastered."

So that's what we did. By nine, a number of my classmates were drunk and dancing. The guys had removed their jackets and the girls had removed their shoes—it truly was a floating bar mitzvah. Adrienne danced wildly with some other girl for fifteen minutes, and Manbuddy fell into a trance-like state watching them. I'm not much of a dancer, but I did dance with Victoria for at least an hour, and though the space was tight, I could tell that Victoria was a good dancer. Suspiciously good. I must have been keeping up, though, because after Adrienne's girl-on-girl dancing broke up, Manbuddy shifted his gaze to Victoria and me.

It was creepy.

"WE'VE GOT A CLASSMATE STARING AT US."

"I'M USED TO IT."

"I BET; YOU DANCE REALLY WELL."

"YOU THINK HE WANTS TO CUT IN?"

"YES."

"THEN I'LL GO TO THE BATHROOM."

Cute.

Victoria left and, before I realized what was happening, Cassandra had taken her place. She reeked of Scotch and laughed at everything I said, even though I wasn't making any jokes.[121] She danced closer and closer to me and eventually I had to push her back a bit.

"I THOUGHT YOU LIKED ME," Cassandra said.

"I'VE BEEN DANCING WITH MY GIRLFRIEND FOR THE LAST HOUR. I LIKE HER."

"BUT YOU ASKED ME FOR MY NUMBER."

"YOU GAVE ME YOUR NUMBER."

"YOU ASKED ME FOR IT LAST SEMESTER. AND THEN THE HUG. AND YOU TOOK MY NUMBER. . . ." She looked like she was going to cry again. "I'M SO BAD AT THIS STUFF."

I saw Victoria returning from the bathroom.

Instead of asking, "What stuff, specifically, are you bad at?" I said, "You're better than you think." Then I returned to my girlfriend.

---

[121] A similar thing happened to me the first week I moved to Chicago. I went to a salsa club and on the dance floor I met a girl named Lucy. She apparently found me spectacular; she laughed at everything I said, even though the only joke I made was an obvious *I Love Lucy* allusion. I attributed the miscommunication to the loud music, but when we stopped dancing and walked to the bar, I realized that Lucy didn't speak English.

Cassandra spent the last twenty minutes of the cruise dancing with Erik. I knew I didn't have the right to think this, but even though I no longer wanted Cassandra for myself, I didn't want Erik to have her, either.

Since first-semester finals, I had been taking two Advil PMs every night before bed, but I had grown immune to the drug's effect and could no longer fall asleep before three in the morning. Instead of bumping up my dosage, I got a Simmons Deep Sleep mattress with a double-tempered heavy-gauge coil system. The first night with my new mattress didn't go well. I got into bed at one and was still awake at two, which was ironic because at exactly two that afternoon I'd been trying to study Property at the bookstore and unable to stay awake.

The Property reading I'd napped through focused on two cases, the first of which, *Hilder v. St. Peter,* dealt with *implied warranty of habitability.*[122] Ella Hilder had leased an apartment from Stuart St. Peter for $140 a month:

> Upon moving into the apartment, plaintiff [Hilder] discovered a broken kitchen window . . . the bathroom toilet was clogged with paper and feces and would flush only by dumping pails of water into it . . . the bathroom light and wall outlet were inoperable . . . water leaked from the water pipes of the upstairs apartment down the ceilings and walls of both her kitchen and back bed-

---

[122] *Implied warranty of habitability:* the rule that says landlords' premises must be safe and suitable for habitation.

room . . . As a result of this leakage, a large section of plaster fell from the back bedroom ceiling onto her bed and her grandson's crib . . . an odor of raw sewage permeated plaintiff's apartment. The odor was so strong that the plaintiff was ashamed to have company in her apartment. Responding to the plaintiff's complaints, Rutland City workers unearthed a broken sewage pipe in the basement of the defendant's building. Raw sewage littered the floor of the basement.

Stuart St. Peter promised to fix the defects but didn't. Ella Hilder tolerated the awful living conditions for fourteen months, but eventually asked for her money back. St. Peter refused, Hilder sued, and the court ruled in favor of Hilder, agreeing that the apartment's conditions were unacceptable. Open-and-shut.

In the second case, *Reste Realty Corp. v. Cooper,* Joy Cooper leased the basement floor of an office building that flooded whenever it rained. Joy Cooper wanted out. Reste argued that Cooper had known what she was getting into when she signed the lease, but the court sided with Cooper, saying that a tenant can claim "constructive eviction" when the property is substantially unsuitable for the purpose for which it was leased.

Nap-reading through the cases, I felt lucky to be living in such a perfect apartment.

That was before my new neighbor moved in.

"I have some exciting news," Isaac said, beaming, as if he had just won a Golden Apple teaching award. "I just found out ten minutes ago. The dean sent out an e-mail. Here, I'll read it to you." Isaac continued: "From 2002 to 2006, the median LSAT score for full-time students climbed from 154 to 160. That represents an improvement from the fifty-third to the eighty-second percentile, one of the largest percentile increases of any law school. For years, the DePaul University College of Law has ranked in the so-called third tier, which, along with the fourth tier, contains schools in the bottom half of the ranking. This year we were ranked as one of the Top One Hundred schools. In fact, we jumped to the eightieth position. This is perhaps the largest jump of any law school in the history of the ranking system."[123]

Whenever the subject of law school rankings or DePaul's Tier 3 status had come up in the past, my classmates had feigned apathy, but upon hearing that we had made the Top 100 list, they burst into wild applause. Isaac put his hands up, settled us down, and then taught us about false imprisonment.

At the end of class, Isaac said that Cassandra had an announcement to make. She walked to the front of the class and said, "For those of you who don't know me—*and most of you really don't*—my name is Cassandra, and I wanted to let you know about a petition I'll be circulating after class."

Cassandra's petition restated the complaints she had shared with me and concluded with: "We the undersigned are concerned students who wish to have DePaul's legal

---

[123] I take full credit for this.

writing program evaluated by a panel of students, teachers, and administrators." By the end of the week, Cassandra had all the signatures she was looking for.[124]

After signing Cassandra's petition, I returned to the Barnes & Noble café and learned what constitutes a prima facie case of negligence. *The Restatement of Torts* defines negligence as conduct "which falls below the standard established by law for the protection of others against unreasonable risk of harm." According to my casebook, to make out a prima facie case of negligence, a plaintiff must show (1) that the defendant did some act or failed to do some act, (2) that the defendant owed the plaintiff a duty to exercise due care, (3) that the defendant breached the duty, (4) that there was a causal relationship between the breach and the harm done to the plaintiff, and (5) that quantifiable damages occurred. In our first assigned negligence case, *Lubitz v. Wells,* James Wells had left a golf club lying on the grass in his backyard. Young James Wells Jr. picked the club up and hit his friend Judith Lubitz in the jaw with it. Judith's parents sued Wells for negligence, but the court sided with Wells, saying that

---

[124] After receiving Cassandra's petition, DePaul's legal writing department added a professionalism component to the grading rubric:

> Professionalism Points
>
> Twenty-five (25) points of the overall grade for [Legal Writing] are based on professionalism, which includes, but is not limited to, conduct in class, ability to follow rules, and correspondences outside of class. At the beginning of the semester, students will be given the twenty-five points. Therefore, students cannot earn, but can only lose these points.

Every student I've talked to about the matter believes the professionalism points grading component was implemented to suppress dissent, though the legal writing department would presumably beg to differ.

Judith's parents didn't prove the first of the five negligence elements. To do so, the court said, the plaintiff needed to have proven that leaving the golf club on the grass was "intrinsically dangerous."

When I had finished reading the case, I stood up to stretch my back. I noticed Nadeeka sitting across the café, noticing me noticing her. I was surprised to see Nadeeka studying at the bookstore because it got pretty noisy in there and serious students like Nadeeka usually studied in serious study locations, like the library or vacant classrooms.

Nadeeka's precise studying location surprised me, too. She was sitting in the chair I had first sat in when I'd arrived. I'd changed tables because the chair wobbled. I wasn't sure whether Nadeeka had noticed the wobble, and I didn't feel a moral responsibility to mention it—Nadeeka wasn't looking out for my safety, so why should I look out for hers? And hadn't she had just as much an opportunity to discover the wobble as I'd had?

Hell, I even had a benevolent reason not to mention the wobble: I didn't want Nadeeka to think I was making some sort of fat joke, which I would never do, even though she was pretty much begging for it every time she used what had become her second-semester catchphrase: "I have a ton and a half of studying to do."

Nadeeka caught me staring at her and made a palms-up "what-do-you-want?" gesture, so I walked over to her table and in a husky voice asked, "So, do you come here often?"

She rolled her eyes. The eye roll ended in a downward

position and stayed there. It took me a few seconds to realize that Nadeeka had no intention of reciprocating my greeting; she had returned to her Torts book, leaving me hovering over her table like a conversational parasite. I really didn't want to tell her about the wobble; I wanted to walk away. Unfortunately, walking away at that point would have only affirmed Nadeeka's conversational dominance by allowing her the unilateral power to end our conversations whenever she saw fit. So I stood there, thinking about how I might win the upper hand.

That's when I noticed that Nadeeka was studying *Lubitz,* too, and that's when a scary thought came to me: what if the chair collapsed and Nadeeka's tailbone snapped? It wasn't an entirely unpleasant thought, but suddenly I found myself imagining a lawyer making the following argument on Nadeeka's behalf:

Ladies and gentlemen, what we have here is a textbook example of a prima facie case of negligence. First of all, we have an omission: the defendant didn't tell my client about the wobble in her chair. Second, we have a duty: the defendant should have told somebody—maybe my client, maybe the café staff—about the wobble, because he was the one who had noticed it. Third, we have the breach of duty: the defendant didn't say anything to anyone. Fourth, causation: if the defendant had told my client about the wobble, she would have found a new chair. Fifth, damages: the fall broke my client's tailbone—

that's how she racked up thousands of dollars in doctors' bills, not to mention the pain and suffering.

"Uh, Nadeeka," I said, tentatively.

She looked up from her Torts book.

"I was sitting in that chair when I first got here, and"— *why am I doing this?*—"it was wobbling. I just wasn't sure if you'd noticed." I paused, then added: "I don't want it to collapse on you."

Nadeeka stared at me blankly for a moment before responding, "Actually I did notice," without any apparent sarcasm. "But thanks anyway."

She politely paused for a moment before returning to *Lubitz*. Again, I'd been left hovering.

"I'll leave you to do your work."

Nadeeka didn't look up, nod her head, smile dismissively, or anything else to acknowledge my announced departure. I took the hint and left.

In warning Nadeeka about the wobble, I hadn't had her personal safety in mind; I just hadn't wanted her to sue me if she fell. I wondered, briefly, if I was being overly paranoid again. I mean, what were the odds that the chair would actually collapse? And even if it did, what were the odds that Nadeeka would fall and break her tailbone? And even if she did, what were the odds that she would find out that I had been sitting in the chair before her? And even if she did, what were the odds that she would actually sue me?

Not good.

Then again, what were the odds that James Wells Jr. would swing his father's golf club at his friend's jaw?

By half past three, I'd finished my Torts reading, but I still had more than fifty pages of Con Law and Contracts to go, as well as a Legal Writing grammar worksheet, a research worksheet, and a memo draft. I took a quick stroll around Buckingham Fountain, allowed myself a quick workout at the Chicago Fitness Club, and took the bus north to my makeshift office in the Drake hotel lounge, knowing I'd be there for a long, long time.

I stayed until just past midnight and then walked home. After midnight, Michigan Avenue south of the Michigan Avenue Bridge is pretty much dead—especially in the winter. A block away from my apartment, a man leaning against the Bennigan's window and surrounded by Whole Foods shopping bags stuffed with other Whole Foods shopping bags sprang right in front of me.

"Stop for a sec."

I didn't. I kept walking, and I heard the guy following me about ten feet behind.

"Slow down, man," he said.

I kept walking, and he snuck up behind me and screamed in my ear, "That's right: keep walking, you faggot-ass motherfucker!"

The volume alone petrified me. He could have shouted, "A plaintiff must show five things to make out a prima facie case of negligence!" and it would have had the same effect.

By the time my heart began beating again, a group of drunken tourists had come into sight, rounding the corner of Lake and Michigan, so I felt a lot safer.

Maybe law school had made me more confrontational, but even so, I can't believe I actually did what I did next: I stopped dead in my tracks and turned around.

"Excuse me?"

"I said, 'Keep walking.' "

The guy was no longer screaming.

"That's not what you said."

"I just said what I said. You want to make something of it?"

If this guy was willing to fight me, I wondered, why was he so shy about calling me what he called me a second time? The man put up his dukes, and I started thinking about what I would do if he actually hit me.[125] I couldn't have hit back because (1) he might have had a weapon and (2) the Committee on Character and Fitness frowns upon brawling with the homeless. My rolling bag made running away impossible— and I wasn't about to leave it (and my new laptop) behind. I also couldn't take a punch from the guy and sue him for battery because no lawyer would take the case. The would-be

---

[125] I haven't been in a fight since fifth grade. I don't remember the events that led up to that fight, but I do remember that it happened on the pile of wood chips next to the foursquare court, and I do remember that Cecil started it, and I do remember that I ended it. I can't say I won the fight, though, because (1) I got in a lot of trouble afterward and Cecil didn't, and (2) everybody in Mr. Janke's class hated me afterward because Cecil was supposedly such a nice guy, who would never hurt a fly, let alone start a fight.

defendant probably didn't have what lawyers call "deep pockets."

Instead of fighting and instead of running, I looked the guy right in the eye and said, "I'm not going to fight you. I'm going home."

I turned around and walked away, slowly, hoping the guy wasn't crazy enough to strike me from behind. He wasn't. He didn't even follow me. By the time I got to my apartment, he was out of sight. In retrospect, I realized he hadn't really *done* anything to me, but that didn't mean I wasn't scared; I was terrified. Only when I got back to my apartment and unpacked my Torts book did I fully process what had happened: the guy had offered to touch me in a rude or angry manner, he'd had the apparent present ability to effectuate the attempt, and I had experienced a well-founded fear of an imminent battery.

I'd been assaulted.

# CHAPTER SIX

## Lawyer Boy

In Con Law, Professor Laurel taught us *Barnes v. Glen Theatre, Inc.* The Kitty Kat Lounge protested an Indiana statute that said that anybody who appeared nude in a public place committed public indecency, "nudity" being defined as "the showing of the human male or female genitals, pubic area, or buttocks with less than a fully opaque covering [or] the showing of the female breast with less than a fully opaque covering of any part of the nipple." The lounge felt the statute imposed on its freedom of expression.

The Supreme Court had this to say: "Public indecency statutes of [that] sort are of ancient origin and presently exist in at least 47 States."[126] The Court, quoting its earlier opinion, upheld the statute, saying: "We cannot accept the view that an apparently limitless variety of conduct can be labeled 'speech' whenever the person engaging in the conduct intends thereby to express an idea."[127]

---

[126] I find the Supreme Court's words "at least" disconcerting; the Supreme Court, if anyone, should be able to check up on the laws of those last three states.

[127] In his concurring opinion, Justice Scalia points out that society prohibits certain activities such as "sadomasochism, cockfighting, bestiality,

*(continued on next page)*

Professor Laurel called on Erik and asked him if he agreed with the court's ruling.

"No."

"Well," Laurel said, "what arguments might you make opposing the statute?"

"You could say that it violated the First Amendment."

"Yes, thank you"—*for nothing*—"but what specific arguments could you make on behalf of the Kitty Kat Lounge?"

"What *specific* arguments?"

Repeating the question, a clear sign of weakness.

"Anything, Mr. Hull?"

Nothing.

"You have read the case—yes?"

"Yes . . ."

"And you can make an argument on behalf of the Kitty Kat Lounge?"

"I *could*."

"But you're not going to?"

"I don't agree with their position."

---

suicide, drug use, prostitution, and sodomy," not because they harm others but because they are innately immoral. Scalia tries to discredit *Glen Theatre*'s argument that the statute was enacted to protect nonconsenting adults (adults who don't want to see nude women dancing) from visual offense by saying: "The purpose of Indiana's nudity law would be violated, I think, if 60,000 fully consenting adults crowded into the Hoosier Dome to display their genitals to one another, even if there were not an offended innocent in the crowd," which at the time seemed logistically impossible but since May 6, 2006, when eighteen thousand Mexicans stripped naked for artist Spencer Tunick in Mexico City's main square, seems more plausible. Forty-two thousand more to go, Tunick.

*Because you haven't read the case.*

"Let's say you were appointed to represent the Kitty Kat Lounge, *hypothetically*—then what would you argue?"

"I wouldn't take the case in the first place. I couldn't argue it in good conscience."[128]

The whole section snickered, thinking there'd be no way Laurel would let Erik get away with that. We were wrong: "Mr. Hull, I must say, I respect your opinion. Your unwillingness to argue a position you find morally repugnant is commendable."

*What the hell?* Wasn't Laurel the one whose syllabus said that if a student was unprepared when called on, his or her grade would be lowered one level? Was Laurel the most gullible professor at the school? Obviously Erik hadn't read the case. But even if Laurel had thought he had, why did he let Erik off the hook so easily? If this were an exam, would Laurel have given him an A?

After class, Erik held his ground—sort of.

"You've never been to a strip club?" I asked, still ticked off.

"I didn't say that; I love strip clubs."

"I don't follow."

"I think women should have the right to take their

---

[128] Model Rule of Professional Conduct 1.2(b) says: "A lawyer's representation of a client, including representation by appointment, does not constitute an endorsement of the client's political, economic, social or moral views or activities," but Model Rule of Professional Conduct 6.2(c) says that a lawyer may avoid appointment by a tribunal to represent a person "for good cause, such as [when] the client or the cause is so repugnant to the lawyer as to be likely to impair the client-lawyer relationship or the lawyer's ability to represent the client."

clothes off for money, but I also think they're not conveying a message when they do. And I think that a state should have the right to restrict stripping if it wants to."

"And you believe in that right so strongly that you don't even feel comfortable playing devil's advocate in class?"

"Exactly," he replied. "That, and I didn't read the case."

He smiled sheepishly. I didn't know whether to believe him or whether he was just trying to further cultivate his frat boy image even though the Dean's List had pretty much blown his cover.

"Do you want to hear a strip club story?" Erik asked.

"I do want to hear a strip club story."

Erik looked from side to side and then lowered the volume of his voice.

"Two weeks ago, Adrienne, Paul"—*that,* I remembered, was Manbuddy's name—"and me went to the Hennington House and we ran into Professor Grant there."

"Who's Professor Grant?"

"Fat guy with glasses. He teaches Contractual Ethics."

"I don't believe you."

"Swear to God. He was at a table, by himself."

"Did he know that you saw him?"

"I don't know. But Adrienne knows him, and she was wasted, and she went right over and started talking to him."

"You're joking."

"Then she motioned for Paul and me to come over and we did. He kept saying how he needed to get home because it was so late, but then Paul offered to buy him a lap dance. And he took it."

"I don't believe you."

"Ask Adrienne or Paul.[129] He bought us a round of drinks and then he left."

"Do you think he's going to mention it to you ever? Or are you guys just going to pretend like it never happened?"

"I never really see him in school. But I'm planning to take his class next year, and I feel pretty confident that I'm going to get an A."

"One more question," I said. "Is your last name Hull?"

"Yes."

"I thought it was Mercer."

"Erik Mercer is in Section 1."

So Erik hadn't made the Dean's List after all—not the Erik I knew, at least. But just as I had had no qualms about autographing Tally Hall T-shirts, Erik Hull apparently had none about taking credit for Erik Mercer's academic achievements.

After our talk, I headed to Legal Writing and turned in my properly stapled memo. One of the topics of the day was interactions with the press.

"As a lawyer," Devenpeck said, "you have a responsibility to answer questions truthfully and thoroughly. And that applies even when you're speaking with the press."

Where had Devenpeck gotten that from?[130] I had to know, so I raised my hand.

---

[129] I did. They confirmed.

[130] Not from the Model Rules of Professional Conduct, which say, essentially, the exact opposite.

"When I see lawyers on TV talking with the media, they never answer questions thoroughly. Isn't there a difference between what you have to say when a judge asks you a question and what you have to say when a reporter asks you the same thing?"

I was asking for trouble, obviously. But I did want to know the answer—could be important one day.

"Mr. Lax, everything you're saying right now leads me to believe that you should think twice about going into law. Public relations might be a better field for you. And I believe I've already answered the question you're asking, and you know how I feel about repeating myself."

I awoke at seven one morning in March to the sound of dogs barking. My building allowed dogs, but I'd never actually seen one on the thirty-second floor. Given how loud the barking was—it sounded like they were in my matress, hunting bedbugs—I couldn't dismiss the possibility that I was still dreaming. I wasn't; the barking, it turned out, was coming from the apartment directly across the hall. It had been vacant ever since I'd moved in.

I knocked on the door. More barking. I knocked louder and the barking got louder in return. I returned to my bed and pulled my pillows against my ears, trying to fall back asleep. I succeeded a few minutes before my alarm went off.

The following day I met my new neighbor in the elevator. The industrial-size bag of Eukanuba dog food gave her away.

"You just moved in, didn't you?"

"I did. I'm Sandy."

Sandy, about forty-five, was the first woman I've ever seen with hair frizzier than my mom's.

"I think you live right across from me. Rick, by the way."

"How long have you lived here?" Sandy asked.

"Eight or nine months. I like it. Real quiet and relaxing, usually."

We arrived at the thirty-second floor to the sound of dogs barking.

As Sandy turned her key, the barking intensified, and Sandy shouted, "SHUT THE HELL UP! SHUT YOUR GODDAMN YAPPERS!" She turned to me. "Did you want to come in and take the tour?" And back to the dogs, "WHAT THE FUCK DID I JUST TELL YOU?!"

"No thanks," I said. "I've got a lot of studying—"

"LISTEN TO ME, YOU PIECES OF SHIT: IF YOU DON'T SHUT THE HELL UP RIGHT NOW, I WILL SLAP A FUCKING MUZZLE ON YOUR YAPPERS SO GODDAMN FAST YOUR NECKS WILL SNAP! DO YOU FUCKING HEAR ME?"

"I have to study."

"Well, if you ever do want to take the tour or if you just want to come over and have a drink or two or three"—she winked—"you know where to find me."

I mentioned that she was around forty-five, right?

That evening I bought a pack of earplugs to muffle the noise, but I wasn't able to slide one into my right ear. Convinced I had asymmetric ear canals, I resolved to see an ear, nose, and throat specialist. I'm not a hypochondriac. I'd been needing to see an ENT doctor for other reasons. First, I hadn't yet kicked the nasal spray addiction I'd picked up during finals.[131] Second, Victoria, who in high school had worked at an ENT doctor's office, told me on our third date that she thought I had a deviated septum: "It's slight, but I can see it," she'd said. "And that might explain why you have so much trouble sleeping at night. A deviated septum can cause sleep apnea."

According to the American Sleep Apnea Association, "Obstructive sleep apnea (OSA) is caused by a blockage of the airway . . . people with untreated sleep apnea stop breathing repeatedly during their sleep, sometimes hundreds of times during the night and often for a minute or longer." I vowed to see an ENT doctor after I had completed Professor Holmes's Property midterm, which was set to begin the following day.

Holmes gave us a week to complete the exam, which meant it would be due on my twenty-fourth birthday. Holmes said the exam would count for one-third of our overall grade. Marty glanced at the first question and grabbed my arm: "I've read this test before."

At the start of the second semester, Marty had joined a study group with a connection to a third-year student who'd e-mailed the group Holmes's old midterm exam, which she

---

[131] The spray bottle stated: "Do not use for more than 3 days," and, "When using this product do not exceed recommended dosage," and, "Use 2 or 3 sprays in each nostril without tilting your head, not more often than every 10 to 12 hours," and, "Do not exceed 2 applications in any 24-hour period," but I had convinced myself that all four of those warnings only applied to those with addictive personalities.

was apparently giving again. The third-year student had also e-mailed his answers, for which Holmes had given him an A. After thirty minutes of weighing pros and cons, Marty had deleted the e-mail. The three other members of his study group hadn't. Upon further investigation, Marty discovered that at least ten other people in Section 2 had seen the answers to Holmes's midterm as well.

Adrienne organized an impromptu meeting in the seventh-floor student lounge among the students, like Marty, who had received the answers and the students, like me, who hadn't received the answers but knew they existed. She asked us if we wanted her to tell Holmes the truth.

"Let's take a vote," one student suggested.

"Fine by me," said Adrienne.

"Maybe we should just let Kimberly deal with this," Marty suggested.

"Definitely not," Adrienne said.

"Why not?" asked Marty.

"I think we all know why," Adrienne replied.

"But this is the exact sort of problem a section representative is supposed to—"

"Fine, we'll take a vote on *that* then," said Adrienne. "Everybody who wants to tell Kimberly, raise your hand."

No hands went up.

"Well, I still think we should say something to Holmes," said Marty.

"Maybe he's right," another student said. "I mean, if we're going to say anything about cheating, we should do it while there's still time for Holmes to give us a new exam."

"Fine," Adrienne said, sensing the tide of opinion shifting. "*I'll* say something. Just give me some time to think of what I'm going to say."

"What's up, guys?" It was Kimberly. Just walking by, coincidentally, like we were all in a law school sitcom. The group froze, then began to drift apart.

"Nothing's up," Adrienne said, gathering her bags.

"If something's up," Kimberly said, "you know you can tell me."

"Just comparing notes," Adrienne said, joining the exodus.

"Just trying to help," Kimberly said.

A third of the section skipped Torts to work on Holmes's midterm. Isaac went over the *Yania v. Bigan* case, in which strip-mining operation owner John Bigan dared Joseph Yania, a strip-mining operator, to jump into a ten-foot-deep pool of water. Then Bigan watched Yania, "a competent adult," drown.

The court ruled that John Bigan had no legal duty to attempt a rescue. Perhaps Bigan didn't save Yania because he was familiar with the *Crowley v. Spivey* case, in which the court said that once somebody voluntarily undertakes to protect another person, the undertaking may arise to a legal duty of care. If, for example, you save a woman's life by giving her CPR, but you break two of her ribs in the process, the woman can sue you for the broken ribs, arguing (1) that in saving her you assumed a legal duty to care for her and were negligent in performing CPR, (2) that if you hadn't saved her, somebody else could have, and (3) that if somebody else had done it, they probably wouldn't have broken her ribs doing so.

I wondered what I would do if I found myself in a situation like Bigan's. Would I overlook the *Crowley v. Spivey* case and rescue the person in danger?

I'd find out two weeks later.


I met Marty and Victoria at Barnes & Noble. Marty and I weren't planning to study together—rather, we were planning to study in each other's presence as Victoria paged through photography books. Marty knew how I felt about studying in groups. The café was giving away free blueberry scone samples, and given that I was their best customer, I felt entitled to three. Marty showed up twenty minutes after Victoria and I had and he came to our table carrying a cup of coffee and a scone sample in a paper café cup. He held the cup out to me and asked, "Would you like one?"

"Sure," I said, popping the scone bite in my mouth.

"Or you could take the whole thing. . . ."

"You just said I could have it."

"Not the whole thing."

"You said, 'Would you like one?' "

"*Yes*. . . . "

"Which implies you were offering me the whole thing."

"I was offering a piece."

"Right. A piece. A sample. One sample."

"No; one piece *of* the sample. One piece of the piece. I wanted you to break a piece off and eat it."

We turned to Victoria, who looked to Marty and said, "Rick is right, on a purely technical level. . . ."

I wasn't sure what that meant, but I should have cut her off right there.

"But"—Victoria was looking to me now—"I vote for Marty because taking the whole sample was a rude thing to do, and that's all there is to it."

*A rude thing to do? Had Victoria even listened to our arguments? This isn't about rudeness; this is about whether a reasonable person in my position should have known that Marty was offering me a piece of his sample and not the sample itself.*

But maybe it was about rudeness. Jurors are instructed to follow the law, but that doesn't mean that they do; jurors go with their gut. Victoria's decision had only affirmed the first rule of trial law: it's not about the legal issue, it's about the people.

Though I'd lost the argument—according to Victoria, at least—I'd enjoyed having it. Before law school, I'd spent hours arguing with my friend Steve the law clerk and with the guys in Tally Hall and I hadn't seen a dime for my efforts. That, I realized, would soon change.

On a litigation kick, I returned to my apartment, took a few Tootsie Rolls from the glass jar on the building manager's secretary's desk, knocked on the building manager's door, and prepared to put my trial skills to work for a second time:

"I've been living in the building for over half a year now, and I really like it here."

"But. . . ."

"But somebody moved in across from me a few weeks ago, and now there's a bit of a problem. . . ."

"Which is?"

"She's got these two dogs, and they won't stop barking, and I can hear them from my bedroom."

"Are they keeping you awake?"

"Some nights, and they always bark in the morning. Early in the morning—like six or seven. And sleep's important to me because I'm a law student, so I don't get much in the first place."

"I'm not sure if there's anything I can do about that. When you moved in here, you did know the building was dog-friendly, right?"

She was saying, essentially, that I had been put on notice. But Joy Cooper, from the *Reste Realty Corp. v. Cooper* case, had been put on notice, too—and she'd won that case. Just as Cooper selected the property for a specific purpose (holding business meetings), I had selected my apartment for a specific purpose: doing well in school. Sandy's dogs, though, were jeopardizing my academic success by depriving me of the sleep I wasn't really getting in the first place.

"The truth is," the building manager told me, "you're not the first person to complain about those dogs. I've had tenants from thirty-one and thirty-three complaining, too. I'll see what I can do."

I assumed that was apartment managerese for "I'll do absolutely nothing and see if you complain about this again," but a few days later the barking stopped. I couldn't figure out why or how, though, so I went back to the apartment manager's office to find out what had happened.

"I just wanted to drop by and say thanks for clearing the whole barking situation up. What exactly did you do, if I may ask?"

"Nothing. No thanks necessary. The tenant moved out."

"She was just planning to stay just the one month?"

"Guess so; she moved out."

I'll never know whether the apartment manager had asked Sandy to leave or Sandy really had left of her own volition, but given Sandy's undeniable (and understandable) attraction to me, I suspect the former.


The day our midterms were due, my birthday, Professor Holmes taught us *Mannillo v. Gorski*. Home owners Margaret and Chester Gorski built a staircase that encroached upon their neighbors Fred and Alice Mannillo's land. The Mannillos didn't discover the encroachment until years later. Margaret Gorski claimed that she deserved the land since she'd occupied it for so long. The New Jersey Supreme Court agreed with her, holding that you can acquire title to property if, for a statutory period, you maintain actual, open, continuous, exclusive possession of it.

Next we went through *Othen v. Rosier*. Albert Othen needed to cross Estella Rosier's yard to reach the public highway, so Rosier purposely flooded his yard to prevent Othen from crossing it by foot. Albert Othen sued for *in-*

*junctive relief,*[132] and the court granted it, saying Othen had earned an *easement by necessity,* a right to cross over Estella Rosier's yard.

Holmes collected our midterms at the end of class and didn't mention anything about the leaked answers.

After class, I asked Adrienne whether she had told Holmes about the leak.

"You didn't hear? We had another meeting three days ago and decided not to tell," Adrienne informed me. "We decided that would be the best decision for everyone."

"We did?"

"A lot of us did."

"Was Marty there?"

"No."

"And I wasn't there."

"Right."

"Did you just invite the people who didn't want to tell?"

"Well, the exam is done now, so it doesn't really matter, but for your information, no, that's not what we did. Just worked out that way."

Turning twenty-four was nothing special. I had been legally drinking for three years and the novelty had worn off. The best birthday milestones I had to look forward to were airport car rentals in one year and an AARP membership in twenty-six.

Victoria gave me a $75 Abercrombie & Fitch gift card.

---

[132] *Injunctive relief:* a court order to do something or not to do something.

"I got this for you," she explained, "because Abercrombie is the one men's clothing store I could think of that doesn't sell dress shirts and ties and I think it's time for you to expand your wardrobe. Seriously, you could take a break from the whole shirt and tie thing."

I liked wearing a shirt and tie every day. It made me feel like a lawyer, and I had come to think of it as my trademark, and I had never had a trademark before. If Victoria and I were going to continue dating, I resolved, she'd have to learn to live with my self-imposed legal dress code.

Victoria took me to a BYOB sushi place in Lincoln Park and told me that I needed to spend less time studying and more time with her. I told her that even if that were true, we could discuss it on a day that wasn't my birthday. She told me I was wrong and that she had been trying to have the conversation with me for weeks but that she was never able to do so because I always had so much studying to do.

"I have no control over that."

"You have complete control over how much you study."

"I have to keep my scholarship."

"You have to show me that you care about me."

"I do care about you."

"You don't show it."

Victoria thought for a moment and said, "No, you're right. It's your birthday. We can have this conversation tomorrow. We *can* have this conversation tomorrow, right?"

"Right."

"Okay then. Topic change. Go."

I told Victoria about Erik's "moral predicament" on the

*Glen Theatre* case. Then I asked what she thought of the court's holding.

"Let me get this straight," she said. "It all comes down to whether stripping counts as speech?"

"Yes," I said. "The question is: does stripping convey a message?"

"You should ask my ex-coworkers."

Victoria, it turned out, had paid for the other half of college working at the Hennington House, the strip club where Erik had run into Contractual Ethics professor Grant.

"Do you want to go tonight?"

"I've never been to a strip club before."

"Yeah, right."

"Swear to God."

"Well, that's going to change tonight."

"I don't know. . . ."

"Sometimes I feel like I'm dating an after-school special."

The Hennington House vaudeville theater opened in 1919, closed down in 1931, reopened in 1935, and then promptly closed down again the following year. It reopened again in 1960 as a mainstream movie house. As the years went by, the theater showed more and more pornographic films, and by 1974 the Hennington House showed only pornographic films. The Hennington House closed down, remodeled in 1986 and then reopened as the Hennington House Gentlemen's Club.

The guy working in the front cage wanted $25 from me and $20 from Victoria. He didn't believe that Victoria used to work there.

"I worked here for two years, and this is my boyfriend. Please just let us in."

"You want me to radio the manager?" the man threatened.

"Yes, I do. Tell him Oracle is here."

Before I could make fun of Victoria's stripper name, she put her hand over my mouth.

After a brief phone call, the man in the cage said, "You guys are good to go."

Victoria led me past the in-house sex toy store—"*way* overpriced," she told me—and into the main theater. Victoria was the only girl there . . . wearing pants. There was an old guy in a Hawaiian shirt sitting in the corner with Asian nurses on either side.

"You know that guy?" I asked.

"Yep."

"Ever dance for him?"

"Nope; Asians only. The man knows what he wants."

"Is he a good tipper?"

"Any guy with two dancers to himself is a good tipper."

In various forms of undress, the dancers walked through the crowd taking drink orders and soliciting lap dances, which cost $10 each. According to Victoria, if a lap dance goes well, the dancer will ask the customer whether he wants a "booth dance."

"You make all your money in the booths. The hard part is talking guys into getting one; they cost seventy-five bucks."

"What do you get for that?"

"Three songs. Most girls will usually touch the guys through their clothes a little and, even though it's against the rules, some girls will let the guys touch them, too."

"Did you—" I was about to ask Victoria if she'd let men touch her, but halfway through the question, I realized that I didn't want to know the answer.

"Did I what?"

"Did you . . . get a lot of booth dances?"

"No. I felt terrible asking the guys for them; seventy-five bucks is so much money. A lot of these guys are teachers and construction workers and things like that, and they just don't have that kind of money to throw around."

"You must have been the worst stripper ever."

"I was. And if you were going to ask me whether I let them touch me, the answer is no."

A comically busty blonde in her late thirties wearing lime green boyshorts and a tight white tank top asked whether we wanted anything to drink. I asked for a Long Island Iced Tea.

"Sweetie, is this your first time?" she replied.

Because it was my first time, I didn't know that the state of Illinois prohibits alcohol sales in strip clubs because, according to the city, the combination of nudity and intoxication would bring about an "undesirable secondary impact" on the communities surrounding the strip clubs.

"Actually it is my first time. So tell me, what are all the poles for?"

"We'll have Diet Cokes," Victoria interrupted.

"Two Diet Cokes. Got it. And if you need anything else,

my name is Star—and that's not my stripper name; that's my *real* name."

After Star left, I asked Victoria whether customers asked her for her real name often.

"Every night. I said that my name was Alexandria, but that everybody called me Alex. The other question everybody asked is, 'What do you do when you're not stripping?'"

"And your answer was?"

"The truth: I told them I studied art history at Northwestern and that I stripped to pay my tuition. Of course, nobody believed me because all strippers tell their customers that they dance to pay their tuition."

A dancer in thigh-high patent-leather black boots, leopard panties, and a lacy black bra recognized Victoria and came over to chat.

"Whatever you do," the dancer told Victoria, "don't come back. Business is terrible. I'm looking for somewhere else to go. What have you been up to?"

"Working at a gallery."

"*Stay there.*"

As Victoria and I watched the blonde give a table dance to a faraway patron, Victoria said, "You know what's going through that girl's mind right now? *I hate you. You're gross. Just give me your money and go back to your pathetic life and come back when you have more money for me.*"

I don't know what it's like to go to a strip club with a group of guys, but going to a strip club with a former stripper sucks.

When Star returned with our Diet Cokes, she asked me what I did.

"I'm a law student. I actually just read a case in Constitutional Law about stripping and freedom of expression. Let me get your opinion on something: when you're dancing, are you conveying a message?"

"I guess so."

"And what's the message?"

Star looked to Victoria, who nodded, indicating I was "cool."

"I'm saying, *Look at my breasts and then give me your money.*"


Victoria couldn't sleep. I breathed too loudly. I rolled in bed. The blinds in my bedroom didn't block the light out, nor did the eye masks I bought. The earplugs fell out. That was the last thing she complained about before falling asleep at five in the morning. The first thing we talked about after we woke up at noon was who was going to shower first.

"Just let me go first," I said. "I have to get my day started; I have so much reading to do. Besides, I let you shower first the past five times."

"I should get to shower first every time."

Eventually Victoria gave in and told me to shower first, so I did.

When I came out of the bathroom, she said, "Why didn't you let me shower first?"

"You told me I could shower first."

"That's because I can't stand fighting with you! You should have figured that out."

"Let me get this straight: You're mad at me for showering first, after you told me I could shower first? You're mad at me for not reading your mind? That's the dumbest thing I ever heard."

I shouldn't have said that. Victoria didn't say anything, and the silence killed me. Brilliant tactic; when trial lawyers get adverse witnesses to say something stupid on the witness stand, they'll remain silent for ten or fifteen seconds to let the witness's stupidity sink in with the jurors. My stupidity sure sank in with me.

Victoria left my apartment that morning without showering at all. She broke up with me three days later.

From the beginning, Professor Laurel had encouraged us law students to argue, and I'd done so, both inside and outside of class, to a greater and greater extent. In fact, I'd grown emotionally immune to the process of disagreement, which was a good thing with respect to my future career but, with respect to Victoria, not so much. A frivolous disagreement in my mind had been a huge confrontation for her.

Breaking up with me, she said that I had put school ahead of her, and that she "wanted to date Rick Lax the human being, not Lawyer Boy."

"You're accusing me of breaking our relationship contract?"

"You see?!"

"That was a joke!"

"How the hell am I supposed to know?"

Victoria had painted me into a corner; the more I tried to convince her that I was Rick Lax the human being and not Lawyer Boy, the less I sounded like the former and the more I sounded like the latter. My situation reminded me of a segment from the 1980 TV special *The Magic of David Copperfield III,* which begins with Copperfield looking into the camera and delivering the following monologue:

> I have a friend who is a comedian, and every time he gets in a tense moment, like with his girlfriend, he tries to avoid the situation by making jokes. Well, it dawned on me that I do the same thing, but instead of using jokes, I use what's most comfortable with me: I do magic. And right now . . . I'd like to re-create for you a real situation from my life, where I didn't take someone seriously enough, and I almost lost something very dear to me.

The lights go up and we see Copperfield's girlfriend in his apartment, packing her belongings into a large garment bag. She's leaving him. Copperfield tries to win her back, through magic, but it soon becomes clear that magic is the reason she's leaving him—she's had enough of it. The more upset she gets, the more tricks Copperfield does to win her back, and the more tricks he does to win her back, the more upset she gets.

My situation differed from Copperfield's in one significant way: Copperfield eventually won the girl back.

Two hours after the breakup, my cell phone rang.

"We still on for the bookstore tonight?"

It was Marty.

"Victoria left me."

"What?"

"She just left me."

"She broke up with you?"

"Two hours ago."

"Oh my God. Do you want me to come over?"

"No...yes."

"I'll be there in twenty."

When Marty showed up, he set a bottle of Scotch on the kitchen counter, gave me a hug, and asked if I was okay.

"If I seem okay, it's because I'm still in shock. Didn't see this one coming."

I don't drink Scotch, but I did then.

"So what happened?"

"It was just some stupid fight about showering."

"She broke up with you over showering?"

"No. I mean, yes, but not really; it was more than that."

"What was it?"

"She said that I put school ahead of her."

"And did you?"

I poured myself a second drink.

"I might have."

I downed it.

"What am I talking about? I absolutely put school ahead of her. I'm lucky she stayed with me as long as she did."

"Did you love her?"

"Yes."

"I'm sorry."

"Me, too."

A third drink.

The shock was wearing off.

I got a B on Holmes's midterm and Marty got a B+. Word got around to the whole section that some students had had access to an upperclassman's answers. Marty forwarded me the e-mail he had sent Holmes: "Some students may have looked through an upperclassman's answers to your old examination." He also forwarded me Holmes's response:

> I find it highly unlikely that students would copy an upperclassman's answers, even if they had read them. I also find it highly unlikely that copying those answers would affect a student's grade. Remember, we don't know what grades the students who read the answers would have gotten had they not read the answers. I'm afraid there's little I can do at this point.

Marty scheduled a meeting with Holmes, ostensibly to discuss his grade. Once Holmes told Marty that he was just two points away from getting an A, he told her everything he knew, except for specific names.

Marty asked Holmes whether she kept upperclassmen's old exam answers, and she said that she did. He then asked her to go through them and compare them to those of the students who'd received A's.

"I didn't think she would actually do it with me sitting

in the room, but she went right over to her file cabinet and started pulling out stacks of papers. She said, 'Here's a stack of all the people who got A's on the exam last year.' Then, she said, 'If you really want me to do this, you're going to have to give me names.' "

Marty sent an e-mail to the Dean of Internal Affairs, who told him that she would only investigate further if he would provide her with specific names. She said that he couldn't keep his accusations anonymous. She also told him to bring the matter up to the Section 2 SBA representative.

After another drunken night at McFadden's, I hailed a taxi.

"Where to?" the cabbie asked.

"To one eight one North Michigan. Wake me up when we get there."

I promptly fell asleep in the taxi's backseat.

The cabbie woke me up and said, "I can't find your place."

I didn't recognize any of the buildings around us.

"Where are we?" I asked.

"Two one eight one North Michigan."

"*One* eight one North Michigan."

"You said '*two* one eight one.' "

I realized I'd said "*to* one eight one," as in "take me *to* one eight one so I can eat a sandwich and pass out."

"Never mind," I said. "Just drive south. *One* eight one Michigan Avenue."

When the cabbie stopped at the traffic light on Michigan between Borders and the Water Tower Place mall, I saw a giant chunk of metal fly through the air and crash into one of the Water Tower Place's revolving doors. What I'd seen was a car's bottom; it had flipped on its side.

I called 911.[133]

"I'm at Michigan and Pearson. A car just crashed into the Water Tower Place, and now it's on its side and it's smoking."

I threw a ten-dollar bill at the driver and jumped out of the taxi to see how I could help. There was only one person in the car, and he wasn't moving. Two pedestrians started to climb up the side (technically the bottom) of the car, saying they were going to try to pull him out.

"Stop!" I shouted. "Don't move him! We don't want to give him a spinal injury. Just wait until the ambulance comes."

"Did you call 911?"

---

[133]It wasn't my first 911 call. When Steve the law clerk and I were ten, we told two of our Hebrew school classmates to dial what we claimed was a "free phone sex hotline": X11-SEX1. On a touch-tone phone, an X is a 9, so the first three digits of the fake hotline were 911. Our classmates took the bait and it wasn't long before the police showed up, looking for the students responsible for the 9-1-1 call. Steve and I hid in the Rabbi's quarters and the cops never found us.

To the member of the Committee on Character and Fitness assigned to read this book, I'd like to stress that Steve and I were ten when this incident happened. I'd also like to say that now that I'm older, I see that there is nothing funny about wasting taxpayers' vital resources.

Also, in the name of full disclosure, I should mention that Steve and I passed notes during Mrs. Feldman's class, even though she repeatedly told us not to. Once she even threatened, "If I catch you passing notes one more time, I'm going to read them to the whole class."

One afternoon she made good on her threat. The notes read: "Mrs. Feldman is the best teacher ever!" and "I know what you mean! She's got a knack for making learning fun!"

Mrs. Feldman was so delighted by our antics that she invited me to perform a magic show at her kid's birthday party.

"I just did. An ambulance is on the way."

They climbed off the car. But then the smoke picked up and I started to get worried. On television and in movies, cars usually smoke before they explode. I wasn't just worried that the car might explode; I was also worried that if it did, it would be my fault that the guy was still inside. I was worried that the driver's estate might have a valid wrongful death claim against me: I had called 911. I had told the climbers to stand down. I, essentially, had led the rescue. I had assumed a legal duty of care.

Thankfully for me—and the driver, I suppose—the car didn't explode. The ambulance showed up along with a few police cars in a matter of minutes. I told one police officer everything I knew, and he told me I could go.

The ENT doctor stuck a video camera down my nose. It was small, but it still hurt.

"I think you may be right about the deviated septum," the doctor said. "In which case, you may be right about the sleep apnea, too, but there are some steps you need to take before I can give you an official diagnosis. You need to get a CT scan, and you need to do a polysomnogram—a sleep study. They used to do those in the lab, but now they do them at fancy hotels, so it's not so bad. Plus your insurance will cover everything."

The CT scan was a breeze; the sleep study was a nightmare. Rather, it might have been a nightmare, had I gotten any sleep. The day of the study, the polysomnogram doctor called and told me to show up at the hotel at nine. I checked in and began editing my final Legal Writing memo, which was due the following day. Twenty minutes later the doctor, who looked too young to be a doctor, came in and introduced himself.

"Well, let's hook you up," he said.

"What do you mean?"

"Didn't your ENT go over this with you? I need to attach a bunch of wires to your body so I can monitor your sleeping."

"My doctor told me I only needed to wear the wires to bed."

"That's what I'm saying: let's prepare you for bed."

"I'm not ready to sleep. I'm not even close to being ready to sleep. I have to work on this class assignment for at least a few hours. Can we start this thing around one? I went to sleep last night at two in the morning."

"I told you on the phone that the study would begin at nine, and it's almost ten."[134]

"You said to *check in* by nine."

"Why would I care what time you checked in?"

"How am I supposed to know? Look, can I have until midnight?"

"I need to monitor you sleeping for a full six hours."

"Don't worry; I'll sleep past six o'clock."

"I need to be out of here by six."

We agreed on 11:15 P.M.

At eleven, the doctor brought a white suitcase filled with unpleasant-looking devices into my room. First, he wrapped two blue belts around my stomach.

"These measure your breathing depth."

---

[134]Again, it was 9:20.

He then taped a sensor to my right middle finger.

"This is an oximeter. It measures the oxygen in your blood."

He attached electrodes to my face, chest, stomach, and legs with color-coded sticky pads.

"These measure your muscle activity."

He applied clear, sticky gunk balls to my hair and stuck an electrode in each gunk ball.

"This paste conducts electrical signals so the electrodes can get a reading. It'll dissolve in the shower tomorrow morning."

He taped a sensor below my nose.

"This measures your breathing."

Last, he taped a microphone to my trachea.[135]

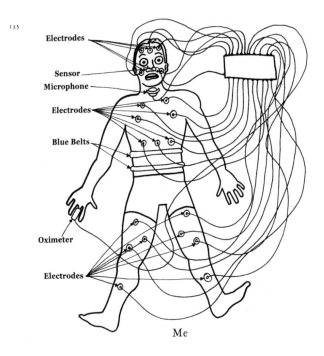

135

Electrodes

Sensor
Microphone

Electrodes

Blue Belts

Oximeter

Electrodes

Me

"This measures your snoring."

"If I roll around in my sleep, are these things going to come off?"

The electrodes already felt like they were coming loose from my scalp.

"If they do, I'll come back and attach them. But try not to roll around."

I lay down, slowly.

"Make yourself comfortable."

*Right.*

I repositioned my pillow and one of the gunk balls came off, and when I raised my arm to reattach it, a sticky pad came off my chest.

"Stop moving," the doctor said. "I'll fix the pads."

"There's no way I'm going to fall asleep like this."

"Just lie down and relax and we'll see what happens."

The doctor walked toward the door.

"What if I need to go to the bathroom?"

The doctor froze and then, without turning around to face me, he said, "Are you going to need to go to the bathroom?"

"Probably; there's no way I'll be able to fall asleep for at least two hours."

"We'll cross that bridge when we come to it."

"Should I unplug everything?"

"If you have to use the bathroom, pick up the phone and dial the hotel operator and ask to be connected to Room 513. I'll come in and unplug everything."

Hooking wires to nearly every part of a man's body and

telling him to fall asleep so you can monitor the quality of his sleep is a bit like putting a gun to a man's head and telling him, "This is a relaxation test; if you don't relax, I'm going to shoot you in the face." I couldn't get to sleep before 2:00 A.M. in my own apartment with my own Simmons Deep Sleep double-tempered heavy-gauge coil system mattress, let alone before 11:15 P.M. in an unfamiliar hotel room in an unfamiliar bed with wires attached to my scalp—the gunk balls had glued my head to the pillow, by the way. So I watched television instead.

At one, I had to pee. I propped myself up on my elbows and leaned over to pick up the phone, ripping off two more of the wires in the process. I called the doctor.

"I need to use the bathroom."

"I'll be there in ten."

The whole process took fifteen minutes. At two, I closed my eyes and dozed off. Half an hour later, I woke up in a cold sweat. My sweat had soaked the pillowcase, the sheets, and some of the comforter. When I was real young, I'd had nightmares all the time. But even then, my sweat had never soaked the comforter.

I called the sleep study off.

"I can't do this," I told the doctor.

"We didn't get a good reading. If you could try one more time . . ."

"There's no way you're going to get an accurate reading. This is not how I usually sleep. I mean, I have trouble, but not like this. Do you have any idea how fast my heart is beating right now?"

"Actually, yes."

"Well, I'm sorry, but I just can't do this."

Even with the wires off me, I couldn't fall asleep, so I worked on my memo for an hour. Then I read a torts case, *Bierczynski v. Rogers,* in which one of two drag racers got in an accident, but the court said that both had to pay for the damages because they were both drunk and speeding and therefore *joint tortfeasors.*[136]

I fell asleep at 3:45 A.M. Four hours later I woke up and discovered that, as I'd expected, the gunk balls did not wash away in the shower.

My ENT doctor called me the following afternoon: "Forget about the sleep study; the CT scan test results are conclusive. You have a deviated septum. Congratulations."

"How do you fix a deviated septum?"

"Short-term: prescription nasal spray. Long-term: septoplasty."

"What's that?"

"Basically, a nose job. Next week good for you?"

I turned in my final Legal Writing memo and breathed a sigh of relief—through my deviated septum. I'd spent about thirty-five hours on that paper—more time than I'd spent writing any other paper in my life. I didn't spend the time for the sake of my class grade, which, I realized, would be bad no matter how much time I spent; I did it because I knew I would use the memo as my writing sample for job interviews.

[136]*Joint tortfeasors:* two or more individuals responsible for the same tort.

"A few days from now," Devenpeck said, "you will deliver a five-minute oral argument. This assignment is meant to replicate the experience of arguing before the Seventh Circuit, so we're going to do it in the mock courtroom. A few points to keep in mind: One, the judges will interrupt you frequently—often midsentence. That's how it is in the real world. Sometimes you can't even get a full sentence in. So you probably won't need a full five-minute speech; you'll spend half your time answering questions. Two, don't repeat yourself. Judges hate that. Three, stay away from the unpublished cases. That should go without saying."

At the oral argument, Cassandra was called on first.

"May it please the court," Cassandra said, "my name is Cassandra Winston and I represent defendant Linque Botique, and I believe the trial court—"

"Counselor," the old judge to Devenpeck's left interrupted, "this is an appellate case—is it not?"

"Yes, this—"

"So do you represent the *defendant* or the *appellant?*"

"The appellant. Sorry. As I was saying, I—"

"I believe you were saying," Devenpeck joined in, "that *you* believe the trial court erred in its holding, and, frankly, this court doesn't care what *you* believe. If you have an objective legal argument, you may proceed."

Cassandra tried to, but she was shaken. She got so quiet that I could barely hear her and she put large pauses between every few words, as if she expected an interruption at any moment.

"The trial court erred . . . in holding that the appellee's

ADHD . . . counts as a disability . . . for the purposes of the ADA. First, I think—I mean, strike that, the 'I think'—first, we need to look to the act itself . . . at forty-two U.S.C. section twelve—"

"Counselor," Devenpeck interrupted, "if we need a citation, we can look to your brief."

The judge to Devenpeck's right said, "Ms. Winston, what must an employee prove in making an ADA claim?"

"That he has a substantial impairment?"

"Is that a question?"

"No? I mean, *no*."

"Continue."

She read from her notes: " 'There exists a difference between a mere hindrance and a "substantial impairment" that qualifies someone for ADA status and I believe,' wait, strike that, 'and the trial court erred in holding that Samir Reddy is substantially impaired. He has shown no—' "

"What authority do you have to support your hindrance/impairment distinction?"

"*Shepler v. Northwest Ohio Developmental Center*. A hospital aide alleged that her employer, the Northwest Ohio Developmental Center, violated the Americans with Disabilities Act by putting her on involuntary disability separation."

Devenpeck set his pen down and put his hand to his forehead.

"Counselor, the first case you chose to mention in your entire oral argument is from the Sixth Circuit?"

The judge to Devenpeck's left joined in, "Correct me if

I'm wrong, Counselor Winston, but *Shepler* is an unpublished case—right?"

"It just . . . I just couldn't find . . ."

"Never mind. Go on."

Mercifully, Cassandra's five minutes came to an end. She didn't make eye contact with any of us as she walked back to her seat. After she sat down, Adrienne said, "Nice argument." I don't think Adrienne meant it to sound sarcastic, but it came off that way. Cassandra packed her things up and snuck out of the room, crying again.

I was called on last.

"May it please the court, my name is Rick Lax, and I represent the appellant, Linque Botique."

So far so good.

"The trial court erred in holding that the appellee's alleged ADHD qualifies as a disability under the Americans with Disabilities Act, in holding that the appellee is 'otherwise qualified' to perform his job, and in holding that the Linque Botique could reasonably accommodate the appellee's alleged disability without incurring an undue hardship."

I paused for five seconds, allowing for an interruption. The judges just stared.

"The ADA was meant to, quote, 'provide clear, strong, consistent, enforceable standards addressing discrimination against individuals with disabilities.'"

I paused again, expecting a question or interruption of some kind, but none came.

"In other words, it was designed to prevent just any

American who struggles to perform her job from taking advantage of the ADA by claiming to be disabled."

Still nothing.

*Something has to be wrong.*

"The supposedly discriminated-against individual must meet certain ADA standards when showing that she is unable to perform a major life activity or that she is significantly restricted in doing so. Samir Reddy failed to meet these standards and, accordingly, the trial court should have dismissed his claim."

A minute had passed by and because I hadn't been asked any questions, I was already halfway through my material. I had four more minutes to kill. I slowed way, way down and moved on to my second issue: "The ADA only mandates that an employer 'make reasonable accommodations to the physical or mental impairments of the employee' if such accommodations would not impose an undue hardship on the operation of the employer's business."

I spent twenty seconds on that sentence alone.

"Counselor"—*thank God, a question,* from the old judge to Devenpeck's left—"are you familiar with *Siekaniec v. Columbia Gas?*"

I was familiar with that case; I had used it in my memo.

"In that case," I said, "the court found that an undue hardship existed when—"

"No, I just wanted to know if you were familiar with it."

*Really? You just wanted to give me a mini-quiz in the middle of my oral argument for the hell of it? Because, that's crazy.*

Still, answering the question took up fifteen substantial

seconds. Unfortunately, that was the only question I got during my entire argument. After I wrapped things up, Devenpeck said, "Counselor, you have time for another minute and a half of argument."

*It is a trap; Devenpeck knows that if I go on, I'll probably repeat myself, which, as he warned us, judges hate.*

"I've said all I had to say."

Cassandra's botched argument and Adrienne's comment following it pushed Cassandra over the edge. She got the Section 2 e-mail list from Kimberly and sent out the following letter:

Dear Section 2,

I know that one of you found out what grades I got first semester and told everybody in the section. It's the same person who told everybody that I cried during my oral argument (which isn't true, by the way; I cried after).

I know that you all saw what happened on the Boat Cruise, and FYI, what did or didn't happen afterward is none of your business.

I know that this has been the hardest year of my life and that I don't need you people making it any harder than it already is. You don't even know me.

Your Classmate,
Cassandra

By May, I felt about law school the way comedian Mitch Hedberg felt about eating a pancake: excited at first, but by the end you're fucking sick of it. I was sleeping less, my back ached more, and when finals came around, I really missed Victoria. If she missed me, too, she had a funny way of showing it: she had begun dating an investment banker who lived with two cats in his West Loop loft. Though I'd spent almost no time with Victoria during first semester's finals, knowing she'd be there for me when I was done motivated me to get through them. I didn't have anyone or anything waiting for me at the end of second semester's finals—not even a job.

During orientation, the serious students had said they wanted to go into the law to help others, defend the indigent, and fight for those who couldn't fight for themselves. The cool kids had said they wanted to join big law firms to make big law dollars. The exact opposite occurred. In a sense, everybody in Section 2 sold out. Because the serious students generally wound up with the highest grades (Nadeeka excluded), the big law firms wanted them for their summer associate positions. When you have tens of thousands of dollars in student loans to pay off and a law firm offers you $2,200 a week to eat foie gras and attend Cubs games, you don't say no. When I asked Dan, who made *Law Review,* which firm he'd picked, he told me, "Satan, Lucifer, and Lucifer."

The cool kids, lacking the grades to work for the big firms, planned to spend their summers volunteering at nonprofits. Adrienne, for example, took a volunteer position at the Chicago Housing Authority. Kimberly headed off to work at the California Department of Justice. Marty, who also made *Law Review,* scored a clerkship with a federal judge. Nadeeka took a job with a liberal think tank. Erik took a job with his father, who ran a big real estate firm in Nebraska. Cassandra didn't take anything. She said she couldn't find a job.

"This was a mistake," Cassandra told me.

"What was a mistake?"

"Law school."

"Are you going to drop out?"

"We'll see."

We saw; she did.

Given my GPA, I could have found a decent-paying job if I'd wanted, but what I really wanted was a break—rather, I needed one. My stress, anxiety, sleep troubles, and loneliness all pointed toward clinical depression.

According to Herbert N. Ramy, the director of Suffolk University Law School's Academic Support Program, "Studies have shown that law students suffer from clinical stress and depression at a rate that is three to four times higher than the national average." Illinois's Lawyers' Assistance Program puts the number between 17 and 40 percent. The depression doesn't go away after the first year, either; a 1990 study published in *Occupational Medicine* reported that lawyers scored the top spot in a study measuring rates of depression in over one hundred occupations. Lawyers, according to that study and others, are about four times more likely to experience clinical depression than the general population. And, clinical depression aside, one in four lawyers will experience feelings of inadequacy and inferiority in personal relationships. An article by Susan Daicoff, "Lawyer, Know Thyself: A Review of Empirical Research on Attorney Attributes Bearing on Professionalism," shed light on that finding:

> Lawyers are trained to be rational and objective. This training, combined with the devaluation of emotional concerns and feelings, can become obstacles to seeking help. Due to their unique personality traits, lawyers may not recognize their own problem until the disciplinary committee comes knocking on the door. Lawyers also have more "masculine" traits, including being argumentative, competitive, aggressive, and dominant, any one of which can contribute to social isolation.

The one thing I found on every Depression Checklist—somewhere between "Are you getting enough sleep?" and "Are you experiencing a persistent, anxious mood?"—was "Have you lost all motivation"? For me, the answer was a definite yes. I'd studied half as much for second semester's finals as I had for first semester's, and I'd found it twice as difficult.

My Property final came first, and while throughout the semester I'd understood that I didn't understand property law, I only truly understood how much I didn't understand when I reviewed my class notes.

*Adverse possession? Easement by necessity? Did we even go over this in class?* It took me four hours to master those two concepts alone, but I did master them— At least I thought I did because on my walk home from the bookstore, I wondered, *If I leave my books at a café to walk around for twenty minutes and somebody sits at my table, do they acquire a property right to the table through adverse possession? If somebody blocks the power outlet and my laptop battery runs out, do I acquire a right to extend my power cord under their legs through the doctrine of easement by necessity?*

Unfortunately, I didn't have enough time to master all the Property topics. There were just too many of them. I only got through three-quarters.

Walking out of my Property exam, I knew I'd bombed it. I knew I'd missed the pertinent issues. Every argument I wrote felt like a stretch.

I got a phone call. It wasn't from Victoria, though. It was from Rob from Tally Hall.

"Great news."

"I could really use some."

"Well, it's great for me. . . ."

"What is it?"

"Wait—is everything okay?"

"I bombed my Property exam. That's all. What's your news?"

"You want the good news or the great news first?"

"The good."

"They're going to play 'Good Day' on *The OC*."[137]

"That's not the great news?"

"We just got a record deal with Atlantic Records."

---

[137] "Good Day" played in the background as the characters received properly sized college acceptance and rejection letters. See footnote 21.

So only after I had hit rock bottom did my oldest friend call to say he had achieved the American dream. Fortunately, I had neither the energy nor the time to be jealous. I had to study for Con Law, Contracts, and Torts. The Con Law and Contracts exams went well—better than Property, at least—and Torts went very well. I walked out of that exam believing I might have scored the highest grade in the class. Professor Isaac had told us that our exam grade would be proportional to the number of lawsuits we could find in a series of fact patterns—the more people we sued, the higher our grades would be.

Here's one of Isaac's questions:

Casey, an ice skater for Disnic on Ice,[138] regularly practices with her partner Vladimir before a public performance. On December 1, 2004, Vladimir accidentally dropped Casey during practice. Casey's lip was cut, her thigh bruised, and her face scratched. Hansel and Gretel, the makeup team, suggested that they could make Casey look new again. That evening Casey performed with a twisted ankle. When Casey landed on that ankle, she fell, causing more pain. At that time, a member of the audience yelled out "You suck!" Vladimir, who had been drinking before the practice, took off his right skate and threw it in the direction of the heckler. The heckler ducked and was unharmed. Gini, a fan of Casey and Vladimir, picked up the skate and hit Heckler in the head with it, cutting his ear.

[138] Is it surprising that somebody who teaches torts for a living won't write "Disney" in an exam question?

Does Heckler have any causes of action, and if so against whom?

"Heckler," I began, "has many of causes of action. I don't even know where to begin." The informal tone was a gamble, but not an uncalculated one. "Heckler's first cause of action is against Gini, the girl who picked up the skate and hit Heckler in the head with it. Because Gini intended to touch Heckler with the skate, did touch Heckler with the skate, and caused Heckler harm by touching him with the skate, she has committed a battery."

Next, I sued Gini for intentional infliction of emotional distress, citing *Slocum v. Food Fair Stores of Florida* and arguing that hitting somebody in the face before a large crowd of people was an extreme and outrageous act. Next, citing *I de S et ux. v. W de S,* I sued Vladimir for assault "because Vladimir had intended Heckler to feel an imminent threat of harm and because Heckler did feel an imminent threat of harm." I also sued Vladimir for intentional infliction of emotional distress.

I sued Vladimir for dropping Casey, and Hansel and Gretel for negligence, arguing that because Casey had asked them to cover up her cut lip, bruised thigh, and scratched face, they should have known that Casey and Vladimir weren't fit to perform. Hansel and Gretel should not have implicitly encouraged them, I argued. Lastly, I sued Disnic on Ice under the theory of *respondeat superior.*[139] What can I

---

[139] *Respondeat superior:* Latin for "let the master answer." Employers can be held legally responsible for the actions of their employees when their employees are acting in the course of their employment.

say? I'm like the sixth sense kid, only instead of seeing dead people, I see lawsuits.

After the exam, I picked up my graded final memorandum from the box outside Devenpeck's office. The memo, I knew, wasn't actually anonymous because Devenpeck had learned the cases on which I based my arguments during my oral argument, so I braced myself for the worst.

Devenpeck's first comment read: "A sad end to the school year. It appears you made no sincere effort." Devenpeck gave me a 0 out of 7 for my "Persuasive Application" section. The attached grading rubric provided Devenpeck with lots of space in which to explain why, specifically, I got a 0 out of 7, but the only comment Devenpeck wrote in the "Persuasive Application" section was: "Just putting words on a page does not constitute an answer or a document. This is, sadly, very poor work." Devenpeck gave me a 2.5 out of 12 for my "Argument Section," and the only notes he gave me in that section were: "You have way better cases to lead with" and the word "no."

A few weeks later, the rest of my grades came in, and all my suspicions, both positive and negative, were confirmed:

| | |
|---|---|
| Torts | A |
| Constitutional Law | B+ |
| Contract Law | B+ |
| Property | C+ |
| Legal Writing | C |
| GPA | 3.133 |

Staring at the 3.133, I realized that I had never calculated what second-semester GPA I would need to keep my scholarship. I had done so well first semester that I hadn't considered losing my scholarship a real possibility. But now the possibility was very real. I grabbed a calculator and punched in numbers. I knew that, after I hit the equal sign, any result lower than 3.3 would cost my parents another $36,000. I hit the button.

3.306.

I had come within six-thousandths of a point of losing my scholarship, but I had achieved my (mother's) academic goal.

I'd made it through the first year of law school.

# CHAPTER SEVEN

## Lawyer Man

They say that when you win the lottery, friends come out of the woodwork to ask for money. Well, when you finish your first year of law school, everybody wants free legal advice.

Violet, my friend Samuel's ex-girlfriend, wanted to know whether she could throw her deadbeat subleasee's stuff out the window (she couldn't); Robin the ex-girlfriend wanted to know whether she could get out of a six-month lease with her fiancé's stickler father (maybe); Borders barista Molly wanted to know what she could do to help her boyfriend, who was on trial for racketeering (*way* out of my league).

Bruce, the Section 2 dropout, had a question, too, and I'll assume he was too drunk to consider the California/Michigan time difference when he called me at 3:30 A.M. to ask it.

When fielding quasi-legal calls like Bruce's, I'm careful to preface everything I say with, "Don't rely on what I'm telling you, but . . . ," or, "We didn't learn about this exact thing in class, but . . ." One would hope for fewer disclaimers from a real attorney, but my friends couldn't complain because, well, it's not like they were paying me. Bruce's call began the time-honored way client-attorney calls have begun since long before my father passed the bar:

"I fucked up."

"What'd you do?"

"Me and my roommates rented this house in Santa Monica for the weekend. We invited a bunch of random people over. And everybody was just hanging out in the living room and getting wasted. . . ."

"How much did you drink?"

"I had like six, seven beers . . . but I had them over two hours. Anyways, I was wrestling around with this guy—play wrestling—and we were pushing each other back and forth, and he just lost his balance and fell into this window."

"Was anybody hurt?"

"My roommate has a couple of cuts, little bit of blood . . . nothing serious."

"Is there any glass in him?"

"I don't think so, and even if there is, he's probably too drunk to feel pain. Anyway, he started yelling about how I pushed him too hard, how I crossed the line, how everything was totally my fault. And all our friends and these random people just kept looking at us like they wanted us to fight, but I just wanted my friend to stop yelling at me, so I told him that I'd pay for the whole thing."

"Then what happened?"

"After all the random people left, I called the owner of the house and told him what happened. He said the window would cost like six hundred bucks to replace. So now I'm sobering up and realizing how much of my student loan I still have to pay off and I'm thinking, I don't want to pay for the whole thing. My roommate should have to pay for some of it—right?"

It was a torts case; Bruce wasn't calling me from prison; he hadn't actually wasted his one phone call on me.

"So that's your question?" I asked.

"Can I make my roommate pay for some of the window?"

After a year of confusion and uncertainty, I couldn't believe the words that came out of my mouth: "I know the answer."

"Which is . . . ?"

"You *can* make him pay. This is a joint tortfeasor situation, which means you were both doing something wrong, and you've got joint and several liability. Both of you were drunk and both of you were wrestling around, so it was only a matter of time before one of you pushed the other into something. As it happened, you pushed him into the window, but it just as easily could have gone the other way around. We had this case in Torts where two—"

"In what?"

"Torts. Second semester. A tort is a basically a legal wrong—"

"Never mind."

"Right, so, in this torts case, two guys were drag racing and one of them hit a guy, but they both had to pay. Your situation sounds like that one."

"And what about the fact that I told him I'd pay for everything?"

"You were there when we learned about consideration."

"My body was in Room 815, but my mind never really left Los Angeles."

"You didn't get any consideration for your promise to

pay for the window. Remember, when you make a deal with somebody, you need a give-and-take. You didn't get your take."

"It's so funny that you're saying all that stuff, because before I called you, I called Kimberly, and she—"

"You called *Kimberly*?!"

"Yeah, and she told me—"

"Wait, she picked up at three thirty?"

"Twelve thirty; she's here in California. Anyway, Kimberly told me the exact same stuff you're saying. She said that, legally, the facts in the drag-racing case were similar to what happened here. She told me that I could easily win this case and that I should call a real lawyer and talk it over with him."

"I'm not so sure about that."

"She said the same thing as you."

"I didn't tell you to get a lawyer. You said the window costs six hundred bucks. If you think this guy should pay half, then we're really talking about three hundred bucks— not six. And any lawyer you'd find to represent you would charge more than three hundred bucks. But that's beside the point. The point is, you have to live with this guy. He's your roommate. A legal battle could make your life a living hell."

"So what should I do?"

"It's a couple hundred bucks. Pay it. Look at it this way: a couple hundred bucks is nothing compared to your student loans."

A month later, Bruce sent me an e-mail thanking me for saving his friendship.

I'm so good.

I've got to stop working pro bono.

Over the summer, I no longer felt guilty about waking up every day at eleven; I felt I'd earned it. I no longer felt guilty about watching *The Price Is Right,* either, especially given that Bob Barker had just announced his retirement after fifty years on television and my *Price Is Right*-watching days were numbered. But I didn't spend the whole summer fielding legal calls and watching television; I spent a good portion of it doing legal research for my dad. He didn't pay me anything, and I'd say he got his money's worth.

I wrote a few memos for him, and he told me they were good, which made me feel proud—especially because it was the first time I had received any positive feedback on a legal writing assignment.

I did most of the research and memo writing from home, but some days I went to Maddin, Hauser. Nobody was surprised to see me there.

"Hey, Rick, when did you start?"

"Rick, I knew you'd come around."

"Can you come by my office in twenty minutes? I need your help with this ERISA thing."

I let everybody down gently, telling them I was there to do research for my dad and nothing more. One afternoon, sitting behind my father's desk and researching online casino law for one of my dad's younger clients, I got a call from Rob.

"We need you for a music video. Where are you? What are you doing?"

"At my dad's office, doing legal research."

And then it hit me: I'd become my father: not only was I sitting behind his desk and drinking from his coffee mug; I was doing his work—literally.

"We're shooting the 'Good Day' video and we need your help for like an hour.[140] Can you help us out?"

*A chance to get away from my father's desk! A chance to reclaim my identity!*

"Yes!"

I was ready and willing to put on a suit of armor or chicken costume or both, if that's what the band needed. I just needed an excuse, any excuse, to get away from my father's desk. Plus, my dad would never put a chicken suit on, no matter how much anybody paid him. And it's not like my dad had rock star friends asking him to help film a music video. Maybe I hadn't become my father after all.

"Okay," Rob said, "we're going to meet you over there. We'll be there in twenty."

"Wait. You want to film here? At my dad's office?"

"Yeah."

When the band showed up, Rob explained that the "Good Day" video concept involved juxtaposing the jubilant life of a child with the humdrum existence of a working

[140] Four hours.

adult. My father's office was meant to represent the apex of humdrumity.

"Should we rearrange the office for the shot?" I asked.

"No; everything's perfect as is. The desk, the computer, the coffee—just right."

The last time I walked into an Abercrombie & Fitch store—this was back in middle school—I'd gotten intimidated and left. I was the only person in the store shopping for Abercrombie & Fitch clothing while not actually wearing Abercrombie & Fitch clothing. I couldn't figure out how everybody got the clothes in the first place.

Reentering the store a decade later, $75 gift card in hand, I wondered if that feeling of intimidation would resurface.

It didn't.

Abercrombie & Fitch had changed a lot in the past decade, I realized. The demographic had gotten a lot younger— I was the oldest person in the store—and the clothes had gotten a lot skimpier. After ten minutes of browsing, I found a forest green nylon shirt with an embroidered Abercrombie insignia on the breast pocket. I held a Medium against my chest. It was too small. I held a Large against my chest. It was too small, too. There was only one explanation for why I hadn't felt intimidated, why everybody looked so young, why the shirt looked so small:

I had grown up.

"Sir?" It was one of the spray-tanned sixteen-year-old clerks. "I think you're looking for the Abercrombie and

Fitch store. You're in 'abercrombie,' with a lowercase *a*. This is the children's store. The main store is on the other side of the mall."

The most common signs of dementia are decline of memory, decline of attention, and decline of speaking abilities. By the summer of 2006, my father's mother was experiencing all three. First she forgot who I was. Next she forgot who she was. Then she stopped talking altogether. She ate and watched television, and if you put your face up to hers, she'd kiss it, but that was about it.

"It's impossible to know how much she's processing," my father said. "Maybe she's clueless, but maybe she's picking up on everything and just can't express herself."

My dad and my aunt spent most of the summer at her place. Their love, for all we knew, was the only thing keeping her alive. But she wouldn't be alive forever, I understood, and neither would he, and that's why I told him, one morning in July, "It's time for me to learn."

My father slung a light brown tie around his neck and said, "The thick end goes on your left, and it should hang down about twice as far as the skinny end. Remember: *L,* left; *L,* long. First, you make a knot like this. Take the long end and wrap it around the knot you just made, like this, and then pull it down through the middle again. Then you loop the long end around everything and pull the end through the loop you just made. Then you tighten it like this and you're done. It's called a double Windsor knot."

For the first time in our lives, my dad didn't slide the tie off his neck and onto mine. He untied it and handed it to me.

"Go ahead," he said.

I nailed it on the first try.

I reclaimed my title as resident Arnold Schwarzenegger at my parents' gym. One afternoon I found myself working out next to an elderly Indian man using the weighted abdominal crunch machine. When the man finished, he didn't fully remove his right ankle from the ankle holder before standing up, which is to say, he didn't stand up at all; he lost his balance and smashed headfirst into the plaster wall. Then he fell to the left, and only as he hit the ground did his ankle finally unhook itself from the holder. The man didn't make a sound, but his face contorted in pain. He grabbed his right knee. His forehead was red. He tried to stand up.

"Stop," I said, and I put my hand on the man's shoulder to stop him. "Don't move until we figure out if something's wrong. If you've got a broken bone, we don't want you moving because you could hurt yourself more. I'm going to run to the front desk and tell them what happened, and we'll get you some help. Whatever you do, don't try to stand up. Okay?"

"Okay."

He was barely audible.

"You promise?"

"Okay."

I sprinted down the stairs to the front desk.

"Some old guy just fell off a machine and hit his head on the wall, and it looks like he did something to his knee, too."

"I'll get an Injury Investigation Report form," the trainer behind the desk replied.

"This *just* happened. Like thirty seconds ago. This guy needs help."

"And I'll help him, but first I have to find out what happened and fill out an Investigation Report form. For legal reasons."

"He doesn't need a form right now; he needs help. He's bleeding. First go see what's wrong and then we'll fill out the form."

"Sir, *we* aren't going to fill out anything. *I'll* take care of this. *I've* been trained on how to deal with this."

I found a different trainer, one who immediately rushed to help the old guy, who turned out to be fine.

The next time I saw the old guy at the gym, he thanked me and said, "You're a doctor—right?"

"I'm a law student."

I'm not sure why, but he laughed.

When Victoria put the chocolates in her purse, I'd worried about accomplice liability. When she told me about the drugs, I'd worried about possession. When Nadeeka sat on the wobbly chair, I'd worried about negligence. But when the old guy at the gym hit the wall, the first thing I thought was, *This guy needs a doctor, ASAP.* Yes, the abdominal crunch machine's design was probably defective—I'd had trouble getting out of it myself. Yes, the machine's manufacturers should

have stuck a warning sticker on the side that read: "WARN-
ING: BE CAREFUL GETTING OUT OF THIS MA-
CHINE." And yes, the man could have probably sued the
manufacturer for a lot of money. But I'm proud to say I only
entertained those thoughts after I'd learned that the guy was
fine.

Victoria was only half right; part of me had become
Lawyer Boy, but I was still Rick Lax,[141] the human being.
But was I the exact same Rick Lax I'd been in chapter 1? It
didn't feel that way. What had happened to my artistic ambitions? What had happened to the kid who played the cowbell
in the banana song? What had happened to the kid who was
supposed to become the next David Copperfield? What had
happened to the kid who brought the synagogue down playing King Achashverosh in his Hebrew school's production of
*Esthermania*? As King Achashverosh, I'd had top billing over
Josh, who'd played Haman, even though Josh was a much
better singer and actor.

Josh never sold out his dramatic ambitions; he recently
wrapped up an off-Broadway one-man show, during which
he recounted the following story:

> My father sat me down and said, "So, Josh, what do you
> plan to do with your life?" and I said, "I want to be an ac-
> tor," and he said, "Well, you better have a good backup
> plan," and I said, "I do have a good backup plan," and he

---

[141] That said, if anybody reading this knows the guy who hit his head
against the wall in the summer of 2006 at my parents' gym, I encourage
you to contact me before the statute of limitations runs out.

said, "What's that?" and I said, "My backup plan is poetry," and he said, "That doesn't sound like a very good backup plan, now does it?" and I said, *"When did you lose your passion for living?"*

Had Josh and Rob followed their childhood dreams and left me behind? Had I lost my passion for living?

I still perform magic every day, though nobody pays me to do it. Besides, the few times I've performed magic professionally were the least enjoyable. Performing at kids' birthday parties felt like any old job—only most other jobs don't require you to stuff doves in your jacket. It's no easier to be passionate about cleaning dove poop off your clothes than it is to be passionate about, as Rob put it, sleeping in motel rooms with semen on the ceiling.

When I returned to Chicago the following fall, the head dean, invited me to his office to talk magic. In his desk Dean Weissenberger keeps playing cards, sponge balls, and a miniaturized "Hippity Hop Rabbit" illusion, which he sometimes performs for guests. Posters for "Ed Alonzo's Visual Comedy Magic," "George the Supreme Master of Magic," and "The Magic Man Starring David Copperfield"[142] hang from his office walls. His bookshelves are filled with photographs of him standing next to famous magicians like Penn & Teller and David Copperfield. I asked him about Copperfield.

[142] The Copperfield poster was a personal gift to the dean from the show's producer, Northwestern Law School professor Anthony D'Amato, the man who gave Copperfield his start in show business.

"I used to serve as legal counsel for the International Brotherhood of Magicians and, during my stint, I spent a bit of time with David."

"Did you show him any tricks?"

"I did. But you need to understand how intimidated I was; I had been a fan of his ever since I saw his first TV special."

*The Magic of David Copperfield 1* aired in 1978. In it, Copperfield did a routine that took place in a re-creation of his childhood bedroom. The room was a mess; there were enlarged cards, colored streamers, and other magic props everywhere.

The scene looked familiar.

After Copperfield vanished a yellow handkerchief from his bare hands, an actress playing his housekeeper barged in: "What happened to my yellow scarf? Oh, look at this room! It's a mess! You should be studying your schoolbooks instead of all this magic nonsense! I'll never know why anyone would ever want to be a magician!"

Dean Weissenberger knew why he'd wanted to be a magician: he got a magic set for Christmas and then he saw Melbourne Christopher's stage show in New York. He was hooked.

"My interest in magic scared the hell out of my parents," he said. "They wanted me to be a professional."

"I know how that goes."

The dean performed magic throughout college, but then he'd gotten into Harvard Law School. "And when you get into Harvard Law School," he explained, "you don't say no."

After graduating, he went to work at the litigation department of a large firm where, in several big trials, he put his performance skills to work: "You could say that I knew how to put on a good show for the jury."

The dean found success in the legal profession, but for all he knew, he could have found even more success as a magician.

"Do you ever regret not pursuing magic?" I asked.

"Never."

"You never think about how your life might have been different?"

"I think about it, but I don't regret my decision. I have lots of magician friends, and some of them can't imagine doing anything except for magic. When you have that kind of passion, doing anything else isn't an option."

I nodded.

"Now, this might sound backward," the dean continued, "but when I went to Harvard, I realized that my passion for magic wasn't that strong because I was able to leave it behind. And now I can't imagine myself doing anything other than what I'm doing right now."

The dean stood and walked toward his office door. Our chat had come to an end. He opened the door for me and said this:

"Who knows? Maybe, you'll be saying the same thing to a student at your law school thirty years from now."

## Appendix A
## The Vanishing Ring

Borrow a spectator's ring and place it
on your extended right first (pointer)
finger. Keep the ring close to the finger's tip.

Bring your open left hand in front of your right first finger,
and quickly bend your right first finger and use your right
thumb and second (middle) finger to slide the ring off your
first finger.

Re-extend your right first
finger as you close your left
hand over it, and then pull
your left hand away, as if
sliding the ring off your
right first finger.

Drop your right hand to your side, and do it naturally. Don't look at your right hand as it drops; look at your empty left hand—the hand that supposedly has the ring in it. Nine times out of ten, the spectator's eyes will look where yours do. Magicians call this *misdirection*.

Slowly open your empty left hand.

## Appendix B
## The Rules of Waterfall

- Shuffle a deck of playing cards and then spread the cards around a beer mug. Moving clockwise, take turns drawing cards from the circle.
- If a player draws a red deuce through eight, she must drink for a corresponding number of seconds.
- If a player draws a black deuce through eight, she must designate another player to drink for a corresponding number of seconds.
- If a player draws a nine, she must say a word. The person to that player's left must then say a word that rhymes with that word. The player to the second player's left must then come up with a rhyme of her own, and so on until a player is unable to come up with a novel rhyme. The player unable to think of a rhyme must drink for five seconds.
- If a player draws a ten, she must name a category. The person to that player's left must then give an example of something that falls under that category. The person to the second player's left must then do the same, and so on. The first player who can't come up with a novel example of something that falls under the category must drink for five seconds.

- If a player draws a jack, she must declare an arbitrary rule (e.g., "no player may use any other player's name"; "no player may touch a cell phone for ten minutes"), the violation of which is punished by having to drink for five seconds.
- If a player draws a queen, she must ask a question. The person to that player's left must respond with a question directed at the person to the second player's left, and so on. This continues until a player either fails to ask a question or makes a declaration. The player who does this must drink for five seconds.
- If a player draws a king, she must pour some of her drink into the beer mug surrounded by the cards. The player who draws the fourth and final king must drink the mug's contents.
- If a player draws an ace, all the players must drink until the player who drew the ace stops drinking— only then can the person to the left of the player who drew the ace put her drink down, and only then can the person to the second player's left put her drink down, and so on.

## Appendix C
## The Napkin Tulip

Unfold a nap-
kin and wrap
it around your
extended right
first (pointer)
and second
(middle) fingers.

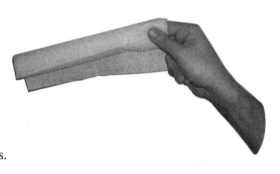

Remove your fingers and hold
the napkin horizontally.

Beginning two inches from the top, twist the napkin into a
compact "stem" by rotating the upper portion (the petals)
counterclockwise with your left thumb, first, and second fingers, as your right hand rotates the bottom portion (the stem)
clockwise with the right thumb, first, and second fingers.

Move your
fingers down
the stem, lit-
tle by little,
twisting as
you go. Do
this until
you get two
inches from
the napkin's
bottom.

Unwrap and fold up the
napkin's bottom, outer
corner (the leaf). Be
careful not to tear the
napkin as you do this.

Resuming where you left off (just below the leaf, which remains untwisted),
continue twisting until you reach the
bottom of the napkin.

## Acknowledgments

Thanks to Rob Cantor for reading through the earliest *Lawyer Boy* draft and offering comprehensive notes.

Thanks to Steve Katz for the great illustrations.

Thanks to Mary Butterton, Kate Schostok, Jeff Schrimmer, Rhea Alexis Banks, Judy Arrasmith, and Glen Weissenberger for helping me assemble documents.

Thanks to my friends and family who encouraged and supported me throughout the writing process: Rachel Sturtz, Elliott Riebman, Susie Sun, Samir Baig, Melissa Salloum, Raj Reddy, Laurel Stucky, Aunt Cheryl and Uncle Marc, Andy and Steven Bocknek, and the Play Group members.

Thanks to my wonderful agent, Melissa Flashman, at Trident Media Group, for believing in this book from the get-go, and thanks to my equally wonderful editor, David Moldawer, at St. Martin's Press, for his spectacular notes, unjustifiable trust in me, and friendship.

Lastly, thanks to my parents, Chuck and Linda Lax, for allowing me to pursue creative projects like this book. But they did more than that; they helped me with this book every step of the way. I couldn't have done it without them.